STILL LIFE WITH CHICKENS

CATHERINE GOLDHAMMER is a graduate of Goddard College and was a poetry fellow in the master of fine arts program at the University of Massachusetts in Amherst. Her poetry has been published in the *Georgia Review* and the *Ohio Review,* and by Innerer Klang Press. Ms. Goldhammer has worked as a writer, trainer, and teacher of reading. She lives in a small cottage on the coast of New England with her daughter, her dog, a cat named Monkey, and a small flock of chickens. Learn more about Dragonfly Farm at www.catherine goldhammer.com.

"Told in wry and poignant prose, *Still Life with Chickens* offers a testament to new beginnings."

—Joan Anderson, author of *A Year by the Sea*

"Catherine Goldhammer's memoir of the year the chickens moved in and she moved out is filled with the noise of life and discovery. . . . With each new coop she built, [she learned] both the limits of will and the boundless gifts of love and art."

—Walter Mosley

Still Life with Chickens

Starting Over in a House by the Sea

Catherine Goldhammer

A PLUME BOOK

PLUME
Published by Penguin Group
Penguin Group (USA) Inc., 375 Hudson Street, New York, New York 10014, U.S.A. •
Penguin Group (Canada), 90 Eglinton Avenue East, Suite 700, Toronto, Ontario,
Canada M4P 2Y3 (a division of Pearson Penguin Canada Inc.) • Penguin Books Ltd., 80
Strand, London WC2R 0RL, England • Penguin Ireland, 25 St. Stephen's Green, Dublin 2,
Ireland (a division of Penguin Books Ltd.) • Penguin Group (Australia), 250 Camberwell
Road, Camberwell, Victoria 3124, Australia (a division of Pearson Australia Group
Pty. Ltd.) • Penguin Books India Pvt. Ltd., 11 Community Centre, Panchsheel Park,
New Delhi – 110 017, India • Penguin Group (NZ), 67 Apollo Drive, Mairangi Bay,
Auckland 1311, New Zealand (a division of Pearson New Zealand Ltd.) • Penguin Books
(South Africa) (Pty.) Ltd., 24 Sturdee Avenue, Rosebank, Johannesburg 2196, South Africa

Penguin Books Ltd., Registered Offices: 80 Strand, London WC2R 0RL, England

Published by Plume, a member of Penguin Group (USA) Inc. Previously published in a
Hudson Street Press edition.

First Plume Printing, May 2007
10 9 8 7 6 5 4 3 2 1

Ⓟ REGISTERED TRADEMARK—MARCA REGISTRADA

The Library of Congress has catalogued the Hudson Street Press edition as follows:
Goldhammer, Catherine.
   Still life with chickens : starting over in a house by the sea / Catherine Goldhammer.
      p. cm.
   ISBN 1-59463-025-9 (hc.)
   ISBN 978-0-452-28848-5 (pbk.)
   1. Goldhammer, Catherine.   2. Divorced mothers—Massachusetts—Biography.   3. Farm
life—Massachusetts.   4. Farmers—Massachusetts—Biography.   5. Massachusetts—
Biography.   I. Title.
   CT275.G5315A3 2006
   974.4'043'092—dc22   2005023623

Printed in the United States of America
Original hardcover design by Eve L. Kirch

For Emma

"There is no use trying," said Alice; "one can't believe impossible things."

"I dare say you haven't had much practice," said the Queen. "When I was your age I always did it for half an hour a day. Why, sometimes, I've believed as many as six impossible things before breakfast."

—Lewis Carroll,
Alice's Adventures in Wonderland

CONTENTS

x • CONTENTS

It Was Never Meant to Be a Farm

I did not have a year in Provence or a villa under the Tuscan sun. I did not have a farm in Africa. Instead, my diminished resources dictated a move to a run-down cottage in a honky-tonk town where live bait is sold from vending machines. But as luck would have it, in a town where houses rub elbows, I came to live at the edge of a pond beside a small forest. I came to a place where a thousand dragonflies the size of small birds fly over my yard in the summer. In a town where everyone knows everything, I came to live in a place no one knows exists.

Five months earlier, newly single and about three tax brackets poorer, I was living beyond my means in the house of my daughter's childhood. A columnist once said that "the lawns are green and the hearts are cold" in the affluent village my husband and I had moved to several years before, in the heyday of our marriage, and I had always believed that he was at least a little bit right. I never felt blonde enough or rich enough or well enough dressed. My husband would have been the first to admit that he looked the part: tall, reed thin, and handsome in a J.Crew sort of way. He actually owned a cashmere jacket. But to be fair, clothes *aren't* the measure of the man, and he didn't belong in Hearts-Are-Cold any more than I did. He could, however, seriously *pass*. Now, a year after our amicable separation, Hearts-Are-Cold was no longer an option for me. The house was too big for my daughter and me, and hard to maintain. But mostly I just couldn't afford it. I had to seek new territory. Smaller territory. Cheaper territory. We would leave Hearts-Are-Cold and our rambling house on its beautiful hill. I would move my fierce and brilliant and utterly rooted twelve-year-old daughter. I was terrified. But I was living off part-time work teaching reading, minuscule savings, and child support. Financial doom was visible at the bottom of the bank account, and other than selling my house there was no relief in sight. So I did what I had to do. I called a Realtor.

And so it came to pass that a tiny blonde woman drove into my life in a really expensive car and became the midwife to my change in realty status, my shepherd. The shepherd— I will call her Penny—was in her late fifties and extraordinarily perky. On a bad day, she dressed better than I did on a high-normal day. On a day when she had to crawl around in basements, she might wear sleek black leggings and a fitted black jacket over a pristine white T-shirt, while I wore what

I called pajama clothes to the high-end market in Hearts-Are-Cold. Penny wore high-octane perfume, but she brought order to my life, which quickly took on the overpowering fragrance of Chanel No. 5. For the five months it took me to sell a house, buy a house, and move, even my little Puerto Rican street dog smelled like Penny. I would become tired of her platinum hair and her perfume, her car and her merry blue eyes, but I would soldier on because Penny was a demon Realtor and she would never let me believe that I couldn't do it, that I couldn't make it, that it wasn't possible to change everything about my life with a stroke of her Glinda-like wand. On the brink of signing the papers that would put our house on the market, I stared at her across the kitchen table. She waited patiently in her tweed riding jacket.

"I can't do this," I said. "I can't sell this house until I know where we're going." Where other Realtors would have told me that was impossible, Penny didn't blink.

"Then let's find you a house," she said.

Finding smaller territory was not as easy as you might think. On a dismal, bitter day in March, yet another gray day in a long string of gray days, Penny and I drove around looking at houses for three dispiriting hours. My daughter was in school. I wanted to shield her. Before bringing her in, I needed to know the lay of the land.

It was the right decision, because the houses were not

promising. The affluent town of Hearts-Are-Cold was surrounded by other affluent towns, and those towns by more
of the same. Houses in my new price range existed, but I
didn't *want* any of them. One of them was pretty inside,
mainly yellow, but sat straight up against a main highwaylike
road. One had a little brook in back, but the inside felt like
the smallest bear's chair, tiny and broken. One of them
looked as promising as a Cotswold cottage, on a postage
stamp of land, but the owners refused to let anyone in. I had
something in mind, a little cottage with clean white walls
and a spacious floor plan. I had a faith born of a lifetime of
finding good places to live: good karma in the housing
realm. I don't know what clicked in me about houses, just
that it did—an unfailing sense of goodness, the ability to see
the pristine apartment hiding in a farmhouse attic, the
beauty in the abandoned home of an aged gardener. I can't
say that my instincts had served me as handily in my choice
of boyfriends, but in assessing real estate, I was gifted.

Now, after hours of looking, I doubted myself. Maybe
where I would live now would be cramped and dreary, with
bad land and too much traffic. Maybe Penny wasn't listening,
or maybe she was just doing the best she could under the circumstances, working with the dollars at hand. Maybe my
luck had turned sour.

"Do you have one more in you?" asked Penny as we drove
in the direction of what would soon no longer be my home.

I didn't. I was tired. The perfume saturation levels in Penny's car had reached the point where I actually wondered if my lungs might be permanently damaged. But my resolve had weakened house by house, and so we drove beyond Hearts-Are-Cold to a town set upon a six-mile peninsula bordered on one side by Boston Harbor and on the other by the Atlantic Ocean. Once the home of a large amusement park with a famous roller coaster, it had developed haphazardly, with recreation rather than posterity in mind. Big houses sat cheek by jowl with tiny ones, shoehorned together on tiny streets. Some of them were beautiful and some of them were decidedly not. The seaside lawns tried valiantly to be green, but they were small, and some of them had remnants of the amusement park in them: an oversized pink teacup with bench seats, a faded turquoise bumper car. Six Mile Beach was a working-class town, a town with a twenty-four-hour Laundromat and a very busy police force. Clusters of elegant old Victorian houses congregated on a couple of hills high above the ocean and the bay, where the views were good and the crime rate minimal. Though in the midst of a slow process of change, this seaside town was the poor relation to the wealthy towns around it. It was insular and protective. The school system was not popular. You don't want to know what would happen to it in a hurricane. I had always liked it there.

The house she took me to was not on the Victorian hills.

It sat at the near end of the peninsula, on the borders of Hearts-Are-Cold and its even wealthier neighbor, but one should not be fooled by proximity. We drove down two tiny roads, past a collection of ramshackle cottages, onto a dead-end lane, and past a brown house. My heart sank as we approached the brown house. My daughter, for reasons known only to her, hated brown houses and refused to live in one.

The next house (gray, vinyl siding) looked sullen and un-inviting on that cold and overcast day, but Penny hopped out of her BMW (black, convertible) and we slogged past a battered monster truck and across the slush-covered yard. An empty house can be a pitiful thing, and this one was empty, cold, and in a sorrowful frame of mind. The floors were worn to bare wood and covered with black stains. The windows were opaque with milky vapor. A demented chandelier hung on a tilt from the ceiling. In two of the rooms, it appeared that someone had turned several children loose with hot pink and blue paint and sponges. Everything. Floor to ceiling. Moldings. It reminded me of a cartoon I saw once, in which a decrepit old man led a younger man down a long hall of paintings. "The next one will knock your eyes out," said the old man as they were about to turn a corner. Around the corner, under the painting in question, was a basket full of eyeballs.

Smack in the middle of the peeling, sagging, dirty gray kitchen, hogging most of the rather large room, someone had built a chest-high, three-sided partition out of wall-board, finished it off with a nice polished piece of pine on the top, and put a rusted stove in it. By no stretch of the imagination was this an island. One could walk around it, but barely. (Workmen would refer to it for months in the future: "Remember that thing in the middle of the kitchen?" one would ask. "Yeah," the other would reply. "What *was* that?")

Then I peered out some sliding doors at a moldering deck. And there, beyond the stained deck and the huge, barren, snow-covered yard, was a large salt pond. The only thing separating me from the ocean was that pond and one hundred feet of land. To the south stretched unexpected acres of pine woods. Such bounty did not exist in this town, and yet there it was. I turned from the windows with a different vision. I walked down a small hall to the back of the house and found two small square bedrooms. They were tidy and neat. The walls wore a blessedly new coat of off-white paint and the floors were wood—the same bare boards with black stains as in the rest of the house, but wood nonetheless. I looked into the bathroom. One could walk into the room only by squeezing past the pointy corners of a huge broken-down vanity. The bathtub was worn down to bare, rusted cast iron. Half the tiles were missing from the walls and floors, and the grime of decades covered everything. But by then I had begun to dream. There was something not terrible about this house. This house was "before" waiting for "after."

Penny and I spent an hour prowling separately in the damp, cold rooms. Our paths crossed periodically.

"I'm thinking this might not be so bad," she said the first time.

"I'm beginning to like this for you," she said the second time.

"I'd buy this myself," she said at last. "I can definitely see you here. What do you think?"

I was not handy. I didn't want a fixer-upper. My father was dying. I was newly separated. I didn't need more stress. I wanted to sit still in a quiet room for a few months. But propelled by I am not sure what combination of emotions, I made an offer. The house had been on the market for a year, but an open house was scheduled for the coming Sunday. I was afraid—and justifiably so, it turned out—that someone else who saw what I saw would come along now. And some-one did, as it turned out, but my offer had already been made and accepted: a full-price offer, which even so was half the price my house in Hearts-Are-Cold would end up fetching. I could not save my marriage or my father but I would save this poor, sad, good house.

We would move at the end of July. I spent the next four months making lists. Lists about money, renovations, windows, skylights, kitchens, bathrooms, gardens, fences, and dormers. I had enormous lists. They were all about hope. I made them over and over.

Friends were polite but largely silent, and I suspected that they talked among themselves about my folly. The ones who had propped me up during the final disintegration of my marriage surely thought that I did not need one more difficult thing. But contractors, builders, and carpenters stood with me in the cold and peeling kitchen. We made plans. We had ideas. We glowed. There was some supposition that they liked the house so much because they saw dollar signs written all over it. But I thought that, like me, they could see beyond its tawdry exterior into its radiant soul. The house was waiting for us—the carpenter, the plumber, the electrician, and the dreamer—to roll up our collective sleeves and bring it back to life.

And so I bought my cottage, my house by the sea. For the five months it took to finalize both deals I moved daily from joy to despair. I had found a house. A house I could work with. But look what I had done, the project I had taken on, what I had gotten myself in for. In the year that followed, I would sell one house, buy another, renovate it, move myself, my daughter, my dog, my cat, and six chickens, and become obsessed with the meaning of life.

It was never meant to be a farm.

This is the story of my foray into the salvation of one sorry house and garden and one slightly tattered soul. It is the story of a small house on a big piece of land, by a salt pond, nine hundred feet from the great Atlantic Ocean. It is the story of a time that began as failure and turned into grace for a mother and a daughter and a small, determined dog. And, in what started as a bribe and then became a love story, it is the tale of my reluctant ownership of six two-day-old chickens who came to live with us here, on Dragonfly Farm.

A Little Cosmic Je ne Sais Quoi

The first and foremost way I knew my marriage was in trouble was the usual way, the trouble itself. But there were other indications, of course, inner manifestations of outer turmoil, you might call them: red flags, warning bells, alarms at full volume. I ignored them as long as I could, and then I couldn't. And so it came to pass that one morning, somewhere in the middle of my life, I woke up knowing two things. That one day I was going to die, and that I had to get out of my marriage. I did get out of my marriage, or we got out of it together, and now, having been through the worst of it, the money wars and other madnesses that come with divorce, it appeared that I had to get out of town as well.

Penny flew into action. She filled out forms, took pictures, and printed a brochure. Small armies of Realtors led small armies of house hunters through our big rangy house. It was perched on a hill, across from a cove, at the edge of a five-hundred-acre land preserve. When my husband and I moved there, in our daughter's sixth year, it reminded me a

little of the town I had grown up in, a small village on a
river, where everyone knew me and my brothers, and
whose children we were, and who kept a loose, benign
watch over us. But Hearts-Are-Cold, I would find out, had
lost its innocence. It had grown wealthy in its beauty and
desirability and I would never be fully at home in its streets.
My daughter had not been born there and had never been to
school there. She did not play soccer or baseball or go to
Girl Scouts. My husband worked long hours in the city,
where my wilder days, long past, and most of my friends,
still were. In a land of boat shoes, in a town that supported
a *really* expensive makeup store, I did not fit. But still it was
our home, and now the Realtors came in and I went out,
doing what I had to do by selling it, never sure it was the
right thing at all.

Just after my husband moved out, in the days when I
thought I could live really frugally and make a go of it, when
I had grand visions of the new life I would have, I decided to
keep a diary. I had kept one off and on for years, mostly
starting a new one on the first day of any vacation my husband and I took together. Our vacations were combinations
of our ability to have fun together and our incompatibilities
thrown into stark relief by leisure and twenty-four-hour to-
getherness. The landfills of New England were littered with

notebooks started on our vacations and abandoned soon after my return to a normal routine.

But this would be no simple notebook. I would model this book after those of Peter Beard, who lived in tents on the outskirts of Nairobi and had many adventures involving wild animals, famous men, women writers, and naked models. He kept legendary diaries, big books stuffed so full of newspaper clippings, photographs, magazine ads, his own drawings, drops of blood, leaves, animal teeth, skins, and fur, that they didn't even come near to closing. And so, in a fit of grandiosity or just a failure to think it through, I decided to keep a Peter Beardian diary. It seemed like a good idea at the time.

In the enchanted fields of my childhood, my brothers and I ran wild in the woods and on the river, hunting down bobcats and snapping turtles. Later, in the streets of my youth, in Boston and Amherst, I smoked cigarettes and walked down the streets feeling like James Dean. I had boyfriends who sent me bear claws and fox skulls and called me at midnight to whisper, "Marry me." By the time I was thirty, three men had invited me to Africa, and once I went, only to be rescued in Nigeria by Lutheran missionaries. There was, in fact, a thread weaving through my life of people of the cloth coming to my aid, although I was not of their kind. I was either emitting involuntary spiritual signals or putting myself into situations in which I needed rescuing. I was probably doing both. At twenty-four I had a lover who studied baboons in Kenya and had a dog called Kika, the Swahili word for lion. I had bouts of poetic madness, played pool in bars, climbed waterfalls, and once my eyes turned from brown to green after an epiphany on the Truro dunes.

And now, all I could think to put in my Beardian diary were photographs cut from decorating magazines, pictures drawn by my daughter, and an Isak Dinesen quote from *Out of Africa*, which I mostly put in for show, a desperate attempt to become interesting in my own eyes, inspired more by Peter Beard's life than by my own. For some reason that would later elude me, I added a picture of Yoda from the new *Star Wars* movie, when he actually had hair and still wielded a light saber in battle. I threw in pictures of Patti Smith at fifty with her long graying hair and bad attitude: *If the people can't stand there, why can the fucking photographers?* But I had lost my attitude and cut my hair long ago.

The life I once had—full of bones and midnight calls, dangerous men who had once been drunks but had quit after driving off cliffs or forgetting their own names, recurring invitations to Africa, and late nights punctuated with cigarettes and poems—was not the life I now had. And neither was some other life, one in which I went to Ethiopia for the famine or raised owls or rode horses like a cowboy. I didn't want to be Peter Beard, but I also did. I wanted something wild or dangerous, something that would leave behind remnants that could be pasted into a diary. But in my marriage, in Hearts-Are-Cold, *somewhere*, I had lost my way. My life stood still, unable to move forward, unable to go back, and unrecognizable even to me.

My husband was one of the best, funniest, and most soulful people I knew, and our divorce would be an unusual one. We would share friends and vacations and holidays and families. We would talk almost every day. I would consider him part of my family forever. But we couldn't live together and we couldn't remain married. The strain of trying had been so exhausting for both of us, and the relief was profound. I was happy to be free. I was deliriously happy. I was so happy I was almost psychotic. But an abandoned marriage adds a certain something else to your life: a mystery, a puzzle, a little cosmic je ne sais quoi. You are forever thereafter pulling out from under your bed or the top of your closet, attic, basement, or flour cupboard a little box. It might be a cardboard box or a fancy hinged wooden one or a ceramic box with a strange flower painted on the lid, it doesn't matter. It doesn't matter because it is an imaginary box, and in it, in it could be anything. A handful of rocks from a beach in Maine, an empty champagne bottle, a photograph in which one of you is making a face. Then, overlaid on that, on top of one kind of fact is another kind of fact, and it is impossible to make sense of it, impossible to leave it alone.

Who was I? I didn't know. I was moving into a little mess of a house, five minutes but far from home, four usable rooms, a deck, a pond, and the deep blue sea, in a town so strange no one person could describe it. I was a blind person in the dark. I was scared. I couldn't wait. Anything could happen now.

Chickens of the Mind

There was one problem. My daughter refused to move. She hated me for selling the house, hated me with all the considerable passion and scorn a twelve-year-old could muster. And while I was a good mother and did all the good-mother things—listened and empathized and honored her feelings—I also used bait. I told her that when we moved we could get chickens.

A psychic once told me that I would have one extraordinary child, and, two weeks before my fortieth birthday, that's just what happened. I never lived on the same parenthood planet as my friends with children who slept all the time and played contentedly on their blankets. I had a preternaturally intelligent daughter who never slept and was happy as long as she was looking at me from the vantage point of my arms. She spoke in full sentences at the age of one, and once, when a friend of mine was babysitting, walking my baby daughter around the kitchen, she paused in front of an Audubon calendar.

"Birdie," said my friend, pointing at the picture.

"Junco," corrected my daughter, and that's the way she was. I have a photograph of her at ten months, sitting with her five-year-old cousin, looking like a coconspirator in a heist. By the time she was seven she had changed her name three times. This was a child who seriously wished to have been called Timber Wolf or Raven or *Bower*. She begged me to pull over every time she saw a hubcap on the side of the road so she could start a collection. She lived for a year with a live snake entwined in her braid. The offer of chickens was sure to get her attention.

I was not a complete stranger to chickens. My grandparents had had them, though I had paid them little attention. I had a boyfriend once who I thought was fabulous partly because he had four chickens. They free-ranged on his lawn and slept in the rafters of his three-sided shed. I liked watching them. I liked getting up in the morning and scattering grain for them. My boyfriend also hunted deer with a bow and arrow, collected his dirty laundry in the bathtub, and watched TV in a torn vinyl recliner. But he was inexplicably attractive to women, which I knew because we had been friends for five years before I actually fell for him when we were both in our early thirties. He dumped me for a graduate student in anthropology who lived next door to his mother. I was with another boyfriend when I petted my first chicken, which was white and very soft. We had stopped at a farm to buy herbs on our way home from moving his beehives. I had known him since I was eighteen. He had a hole in the vivid green of one of his irises. He wore black Chinese slippers and was so handsome that I would never in my life quite get over the way he looked. He too would break my heart. He would break it right in half.

I had wanted chickens for a long time, along with a goat or two, but my husband—who had put up with, but not been happy about, cats, dogs, gerbils, snakes, and fish—had drawn the line at livestock, and I figured I better not push it. So maybe I was dredging something up here, some bits of my past. Maybe it was not about the chickens but about the woman who had been the girl to whom someone had sent bear claws and hawk skulls. So, on my own now, with only my own choices to make, I looked forward to chickens. I don't know what I thought. They were hypothetical chickens. Chickens of the mind. Of the future.

But my daughter seized upon the promise of chickens with the kind of delirium I should have expected—the same delirium that preceded the snake, the gerbils, the cat, the dogs, and the fish. Delirium that gave way to Internet searches, library research, and catalog requests. The day the Murray McMurray poultry catalog appeared in our mailbox was a good day for my daughter. It was the beginning of a logistical nightmare for me.

The Murray McMurray poultry catalog makes for fine reading, and ours quickly became battered, torn, and water-stained. Chickens come in a bewildering array of breeds, and Murray McMurray seemed to sell them all. Cochins, frizzles, silkies, brahmas. Crevecoeurs, sultans, houdans, Polish. Sumatras, dorkings, lakenvelders, fayoumis. Chickens with yellow skin, white skin, or black skin. Chickens with four toes or five. Chickens with naked necks, beards, boots, muffs, crests, feathered legs, plain legs, curly feathers, and feathers as soft as silk. You could choose chickens by temperament (docile, flighty, or aggressive), egg color (white, brown, or blue), and size (bantam, standard, or giant). You could choose chickens with turquoise earlobes.

One could buy many chickens of a single breed, but Murray McMurray also sold assortments. Clean Legged, Cochin, and Feather Footed Assortments. The Rare Breed Special, the Rarest of Rare Assortment, and, for the admirers of the crested breeds, the Top Hat Special. For fishermen there was the Fly Tyer's Special, and for the hungry, the Barbeque Special, the Frying Pan Special, and the Meat-N-Egg Combo: "Nothing tastes better than something you have grown yourself." The Barnyard Combination gave one the opportunity to select a package tailored to one's specific poultry needs. Your choice of two geese, seven ducks, and seven turkeys; or nine ducks and six turkeys; or six ducks and six geese. You could go for broke and purchase the Homesteader's Delight: a package deal containing two ducks, two geese, two turkeys, and ten chickens. Price: $42.40.

Even as I flipped through it, and looked at the pictures,

my heart was sinking. Before giving the Murray McMurray poultry catalog to one's child, one should know that the text on each bird is accompanied by photographs of chicks. Tiny little fluff-ball chicks. Chicks with little poof-balls on the tops of their puffy little soon-to-be-crested heads. Chicks with stripes, polka dots, and patches. Spurred on by these photos, my daughter gathered the ammo she would need to achieve her secret goal. She found a Web site, called Back-yard Chickens, which featured a bulletin board addressing all possible chicken concerns. Someone called "Wes in Texas" was one of the respected elders of this tribe, and my daughter began to quote him frequently. The quotes all led in one direction.

"Wes in Texas says that it is better to get chicks in the spring."

"Wes in Texas says that if we get them in the spring they will be laying by the fall."

"Wes in Texas says that when we move in July we will need to give the chickens extra vitamins."

All over the country, people were preparing for the spring arrival of the cute little puffballs pictured in the poultry cat-alogs of America, and so, apparently, was my daughter.

I didn't want them yet. I was trying to keep my house in pristine condition for the Realtors and the prospective buy-ers they ushered in and out several times a day. Each morning I got up and vacuumed. I made beds and cleaned the kitchen. I polished the teakettle until I could see myself in it. I plumped pillows. I fluffed. I lived with an anxiety level so high that a stray piece of string on the family room carpet froze me in my tracks. I bought fresh flowers almost every day. Yellow tulips. Red primroses in cute little pots. I deadheaded pansies. I worried. I cleaned closets. I didn't want to add six chickens to the list of things I would have to move in July. I wanted to be a painting, *Still Life with Woman*, in which I stood undecided, looking down, stalled and motionless, holding a vase of tulips.

I knew I should say no. I was being pressured, manipulated even, and I was developing resentments. I was being fed the oldest line in the children's guide to getting the pets you want: "I'll take care of them." I was years beyond buying it, but it's a good line, and children know it. She didn't play the guilt card, but I felt it anyway, lurking in the shadows of the impending move to the "gray plastic house," and in the beloved home I was making her leave. Under the weight of this guilt, knowing it was a really bad idea, knowing I was being a wuss, I caved. The puffballs would arrive in the spring and would move with us in July.

Getting chickens at any time is a monumental decision. Doing so when preparing to move a household and renovate a house was a decision so strange that it would never make sense to me, not in hindsight, not ever. But having overcome that hurdle, quantities were a slightly shocking though ultimately minor negotiation. My daughter wanted twenty-five chickens. Twenty-five! For each twenty-five chicks we ordered from Murray McMurray, they would give us a "free surprise gift: rare and exotic chick: beautiful and unusual." My daughter wondered what our gift would be. I had been thinking in the vicinity of perhaps three chickens. She lobbied for ten. I countered with four. We settled on six, since, according to her, three would probably die.

Since Murray McMurray's smallest shipment was twenty-five, another extensive Internet search ensued, yielding all the chick-selling granaries in Massachusetts. A telephone campaign produced information regarding vaccinations, minimum orders, and location. At last we located a reasonably local grain store that offered an acceptable variety of vaccinated breeds. I was not yet conversant in breed characteristics. To me there were still only two kinds of chickens: normal—your average chicken—and abnormal—anything with a hat, a naked neck, or booties. I let her pick.

She made the call, I supplied the credit card, and it was done. The chicks were due in mid-May. They would live in the downstairs bathtub. I had dim recollections of hundreds of yellow chicks being kept warm in the downstairs bathroom of my grandfather's house. My bathroom was considerably smaller than his, and the bathtub in question was the only one in the house. My daughter would sacrifice baths, which she loved, for chickens. I was a tiny bit impressed.

Two weeks before the chicks' scheduled arrival, she began to call me whenever she was out. From school, from friends' houses, from riding and voice lessons the calls poured in.

"Did the call come?"

"It has to come today."

"I can't believe it didn't come."

When she started a weeklong school internship working with orphaned birds at a local wildlife center, she began to worry about Exotic Newcastle Disease, which can be transmitted from wild avians to domestic ones. There followed a third flurry of Internet activity. The next morning I found her carrying her work shoes in a plastic bag from the hall closet to the back door, where she put them on in the driveway.

"What are you doing?" I asked her.

"Practicing bio-security," she said.

As for me, I practiced negative thinking every day. "I should have said no. This is a really bad idea. I have enough to do. I could change my mind!" It would have been understandable. Since placing our order for the chicks, a buyer had appeared for our house. Inspections and negotiations were under way, Penny in firm command. I prayed that the chickens would not come too soon. I imagined the prospective buyers showing up unannounced and finding the downstairs bathroom already occupied. I felt the burden of those chickens acutely, and I was already a little bit mad at them, my daughter, and myself. For a billion reasons I *should* have changed my mind. But I didn't. It may have been that I was taking a belated stand against my husband. It may have been that I was reclaiming a piece of myself. A part of me wanted those chickens. For better or for worse, I was on board, already in tow.

As for my friends, they couldn't believe what I was doing. I knew that in their eyes, though they were kind enough not to say so, I was being a pushover. I was giving in to my daughter rather than taking care of myself. I knew that neither Oprah nor Dr. Phil would approve. I could just hear Phil. "Do you *really* think . . . that giving in to her . . . is going to help her become the person you want her to be?" Only my family, oddly enough, was supportive. "It will be a distraction," said my father. "It will be good for her." As for my husband, he, like me, was relieved to be free of the stress of our last days. He didn't seem to mind about the chickens one bit.

My daughter wrote instructions for me in the event that The Call came while she was not home. And when it did, on the last day of her internship, I took out my list.

I had to "spritz feeder liberally with vinegar, then hydro-

gen peroxide. Wait. Wipe down well with paper towel."
I did.

I had to "hang brooder light 20 inches from floor of box. DON'T HANG BY CORD!!! Use rope. Turn on light and insert thermometer into brooder. It should read about 95 degrees. If not, move light up or down, until desired temp is reached. Keep an eye on temp. Make sure no windows are open." Done.

Except for the brooder light, the instructions were easy enough to follow, though it was perhaps a glimpse of things to come that I was the one who ended up implementing them. The light had to hang right over the middle of the bathtub, and I couldn't get a hook into the ceiling. So I created an ingenious, if bizarre, rig involving twelve feet of fine-gauge steel chain, s-hooks, and screw eyes. I felt proud of myself. I did not know yet that this was only the first of many bizarre and ingenious contraptions that would be required of me by chickens. The temperature rose to 95 in a jiffy and then slightly above. I adjusted the chain. Perfect.

I fetched my daughter from the wildlife center. She came home, showered in the non-chicken-related bathroom, changed clothes, and put on uncontaminated shoes. My life would never be the same.

Actual Chickens

On the way to the granary, an endless hour's worth of winding roads in a vaguely southerly direction, we discussed names, got lost once, and wondered where the chickens would live after they got too big for the bathtub. One may correctly assume that it was already late to be thinking of that. One thinks of chicks remaining chicks for some time, but they don't. I didn't know it at the time, but keeping up with their housing needs would become as time-consuming as keeping up with my own.

As for names, I liked a mix of literary and cinematic. I liked Jezebel, Tallulah, O'Hara, Virginia, Jane, and Gertrude. My daughter, not surprisingly, didn't like any of these. I had once held some sway in choices of pet names. I had convinced her not to name our cat Candy or our dog Connie and persuaded her to accept Monkey and Lily in their place. But no longer. She told me that I would only get to name three of the chicks. I was favoring Tallulah, Jezebel, and O'Hara when we crossed the railroad tracks and found ourselves at the feed store.

We introduced ourselves to the woman at the counter, and she produced a form that listed the number and kinds of chicks we had ordered. Two Rhode Island Reds, one Black Sex Link, one Silver Laced Wyandotte, one Araucana, and one Light Brahma. I had no idea what any of these were. The woman led us to the back room, where hundreds of chicks peeped and chirped from cages, boxes, and cartons. I was unprepared for the effect the chicks would have on me. I was possessed by greed. One box held dozens of bantam chicks. A bantam is half the size of a regular, or standard, chicken, and their teensy chicks can walk right through the holes in two-by-two chicken wire. They weren't on our list.

"Let's get some of those," I said to my daughter.

"Some of those are roosters," she said. Okay, I thought, let's not.

In the box next to them milled a collection of light brown chicks, some with stripes, some dark brown.

"We have to have those," I cried.

"Which?"

"Those! That one! The one with the brown stripe."

"A lot of them have brown stripes."

"That one there!"

She rolled her eyes.

As it turned out, the striped chicks were Araucanas, a Chilean breed known for its green and blue eggs, and we were signed up for one. I asked our salesperson if they were all hens.

"Theoretically," she said.

Having lost sight of the one I initially wanted, I selected a dark brown chick with no stripe. My daughter picked the rest, and soon our little collection was complete. They were all tiny except for the Light Brahma, a fuzzy yellow chick that towered over the others like an addled duckling.

At the register, another customer forked over seven dollars for the contents of a small cardboard box that was emitting baby poultry noises. We looked. Six turkey chicks. He said that he had already named two of them.

We excitedly asked what their names were.

"Thanksgiving and Christmas," he said. As for ours, three had names, silly ones, just what I was afraid of: Brownie, Little Black, and Big Yellow. I was responsible for them all.

On the way home, my daughter stared into the box and worried that the chicks were eating the pine shavings, an activity that could, apparently, cause something called an impacted crop, the treatment of which seemed to involve either mineral oil and yogurt or vinegar and molasses. But all the crops were fine when we got home. The brooder was nice and warm, steady at 95 degrees. We put them in. They ate the Purina starter feed and drank the water. Touchdown.

Chicks have simple needs: food, water, shelter, heat. A content chick, I read in Murray McMurray, strolls around busily in all parts of the brooder. Chicks that are too hot retreat to the edges, and those that are too cold huddle under the lamp. For the most part ours seemed to be content, but we quickly became worried about Little Black, who slept a lot, splayed on the newspaper like a miniature oil spill. I wasn't so sure she would come to a positive end.

Every month, on the occasion of the full moon, three friends and I met at my house and drove to the beach with a thermos of apple cinnamon tea and our dinners. It was my friend Scarlet's idea originally, for Scarlet was full of ideas. We started one fall and soon found ourselves at the beach every month. Even in subzero and windy conditions we'd step out of the car and stand for a few minutes with our tea. A few minutes was all we could stand in those colder months, and as dinner was not possible on the beach, in the winter we ate in restaurants. Our spirits were high on those cold nights, and we were popularly assumed to be drunk, though we were not. Two of us, Scarlet and Martha, were stylish dressers, even on frigid days. The other two, Sage and I, were not, and would, if needed, wear a spare sweatshirt as a scarf or hat. In the winter Scarlet dressed in layers so profound that she appeared to gain two hundred pounds when fully garbed.

After the first winter, it seemed like nothing to keep going in the spring and summer and fall, and then again into winter. We went rain or shine, whether the moon was huge and orange and cast what we liked to call lambent light across the ocean, or was hidden behind the clouds, visible only to the hearts of the determined. It was these women I told first about my decision to move, and these women who were there the day my offer was accepted on the house in Six Mile Beach. Now the Moon Women came on the day the chicks took up residence in the bathtub, and when they peered in at Little Black I could tell they did not have high hopes for her.

"What do you think about that one?" muttered Scarlet.

"Hmm," said Sage.

"Doesn't look good," said Martha.

We went off to the beach and dinner, but I left my cell phone on, ready to get the sad call at any time. The moon was just past full, and though the day had been cold, the on-shore wind felt warm and everything smelled good, of low tide and seaweed. We walked on the beach, then went to the Thai restaurant, where the menu featured Yummy Salad and the owners bowed when dinner was over. I called home. Little Black had rallied, and by the time we returned she was wandering around, eating and drinking. She was still laying down frequently, but looking more like a chicken and less like an ink blot.

Aside from what I picked up from the boyfriends, I had very few preconceptions about chickens. I hadn't had many preconceptions about children either, before I had one. I figured everything would be the same; there would just be a baby around. No big deal. But I was wrong then, really wrong, and I was wrong now. Chicks, while they are not the major upheaval of a baby, do create a minor havoc. You think about them. You check on them. You worry about them. You watch them. You are surprised at them. They grow on you. They drag you onward, into motion.

The chicks looked like small potatoes covered with dust. Their legs, feet, and heads were too large for their bodies. They weighed next to nothing. A gram of down and two of energy. But all together they created a commotion in our house. My daughter and I were excited, but afraid something bad would happen. The dog was either very concerned about them or wanted to eat them. The cat definitely wanted to eat them. But I decided not to think about all of that. Tomorrow was another day.

That night, my daughter vowed to get up every hour to check on the chicks. I gave her a timer. When I woke up the next morning I was pretty sure she hadn't gotten up at all, and indeed she had woken up, turned off the alarm, and fallen back to sleep. She had no recollection of any of it. Nevertheless, all was well. Little Black had made it through the night. Friends came over and held the chicks. Classical music played nonstop in the bathroom, which felt like an overheated sauna. It had become clear that the dog was not at all concerned about their welfare. She sat beside the tub, wagging her tail and whimpering in the way she did when she had cornered a squirrel under the hemlocks. She studied the brooder and the wire lid. I had to hold on to her to keep her from leaping into the bathtub. I started to have some difficult feelings about my dog because of this. I was jealous of people who had non-chicken-chasing dogs, dogs who let chickens walk all over them. Life suddenly seemed fraught with perils.

By day two, the bathroom was definitely too hot. The chicks were sticking to the edges of the brooder like lint. Later in the day they started to pant. We moved the lamp as high as it would go. I opened the bathroom door for a while, ignoring my daughter's dire warnings against drafts. Although the thermometer now read 85 degrees, theoretically 10 degrees too cool, the magi of Backyard Chickens told us to trust the chicks, not the technology. And so we did. They stopped panting. They got busy again. All of them looked suspiciously like survivors.

In between my daily obligations I sat with my hand in the brooder, letting the chicks get used to my presence. Big Red was the only one who was not at all afraid of me. She let me pet her. She also trained her clever little eyes on the top of the brooder, where it was open to let my arm in. You could see that she was plotting. Her sister, whose formal name was Sassafras but who was commonly known as Little Red, was plotting too. They looked like velociraptors.

Names were again a topic of conversation. We were trying to think outside the box. Beyond Big Yellow and Little Black, Speckles, Brownie, Big Red, and Little Red. I tried to fit my original list of names onto them and couldn't. My daughter's friend J. came over and was a veritable font of names, many of them involving candy bars. Every ten seconds she had a suggestion.

"How about Riley? How about Cherry? How about Amy? How about Heath Bar?"

"How about Peanut Brittle? How about Rosie? How about Sally? How about M&M's?"

"How about Reba? How about Chiclet? How about Sabrina? How about Starburst?"

We tried to tell her that this seemed to be a more classic group of chickens needing names with a certain refinement. My daughter considered naming Little Black Sky or Midnight. I preferred Jane, but I kept my mouth shut.

By day five, classical music had been playing in the bathroom for five solid days and nights. My friend Lee refused to wash her hands in my sink. The bathroom was beginning to smell, even though my daughter dutifully cleaned and sanitized the brooder and the water and feed dishes every day. The chicks went about their little chicken lives, eating and drinking and pecking. When I picked them up they settled into the hammock I made of my shirt and went to sleep. Their beady little eyes drooped and closed and they leaned their little heads against my thumb. Chickens are masters at living in the moment. I should stop worrying about them, I told myself. I should bow to their greater wisdom.

They had little tail feathers and their first tiny wing feathers. And they could fly. We are not used to seeing adult chickens fly, and most of them don't like to much, but the babies do. The bathroom turned into a kind of airport, a frenzy of anxiety, with arrivals and departures, emergency landings, skids and slides, and falls into the nether land between the brooder and the bathtub.

On day eight I would drive to Connecticut to visit my nephew. I would be away for twenty-eight hours. When I got back the chicks would be noticeably bigger. Big Yellow would have feathers on her legs. The two Reds would have tiny lines of feathers coming in on the backs of their necks. Little Black would be rangy and bold. The bathroom floor would be covered with chicken feed and grit and bedding and paper towels. I would feel like I had moved to the moon.

Change loomed on the horizon. The house inspections were complete. Blessedly and unbelievably, the couple who would buy our house would not ask to see it again until the day of the closing. I would see them occasionally, walking in the reservation, but they didn't know who I was and I pretended not to know them. I had entered a small window of freedom. The house would be sold and I could stop vacuuming. The buyers wanted a late-summer closing, which gave me some breathing room, and for just this little while I could pretend that we really still lived there, that we didn't have to move, and that having poultry in the bathtub was normal. If not for the chicks, I could have lapsed into inertia, but I had been commandeered by their relentless will to live.

They were going to outgrow their brooder by the end of the week. It was too cold to move them outside. So my soon-to-be ex-husband, who was all for the chickens as long as he didn't have to live with them, and whose job it was to assist with housing projects, got a refrigerator box that we squeezed through the front door and into the room we referred to as the library because it was so long and narrow that only bookcases—and, it turned out, a refrigerator box—would fit in there. This was where the chickens would make their next home, and where I, armed with a large roll of duct tape, a utility knife, and a roll of hardware cloth, would create it. I had in mind a large airy abode, with ample windows and perches. It would be clean and attractive, as attractive as a refrigerator box could be, the Waldorf School of chicken pens.

My standards were high and my skill set low. My first problem was the hardware cloth, which is grossly misnamed; it is a heavy wire screening with half-inch mesh. Since I was cutting each little square individually, working with the wire-cutting section of tiny bead pliers, it seemed that this activity would go on forever. Each snip took several seconds, amounting to about ten snips per minute, for hundreds, maybe even thousands, of snips. Not too much later in my life as a caretaker of chickens, I would graduate to fifteen-inch tin snips and hack great swaths of hardware cloth without batting an eyelash, but those happy days were still in my future. For now, it was me, the pliers, and a lot of hardware cloth, because I had decided that they should have a door, a side window, and a sunroof, and that one whole end of the box should be windowed. I measured and cut the hardware cloth, one painstaking snip at a time. The utility knife worked fine for the box, though my cuts were not as tidy as I had hoped.

Problem number two was the duct tape, which has met its match in hardware cloth and will *not* hold an eighteen-by-twenty-four-inch piece of it to a refrigerator box. About a mile of silver tape later, the new chicken pen resembled a homemade spacecraft, but was still only marginally sound. It was neither tidy nor attractive, but it was big and did have a lot of windows. The chickens would never realize how shaky it was or how they could, with minimal effort, escape. We lined it with newspaper, poured in some pine shavings, added the food and water, and transferred the chicks, one by one, to their new home. They ran around and flapped and flew. We smiled. I congratulated myself. Little did I know that in my life with chickens, I would ever be one step behind their housing needs.

And so the chicken chores moved into the library and filled it. When we got the chicks I had told my daughter that she would have to do all the day-to-day care and pay for their needs. She did the chores religiously every morning, noon, and night. She was a good chicken mama. She was smart and responsible, and knowledgeable, and she loved them. She was also meticulous about paying until she ran out of money. Chickens are not a cheap proposition. The low per-chicken start-up cost was misleading. At $1.50 a chick, and a few bucks for bedding and food, you think you are getting away with something. You think you have discovered the bargain buy of the farm world. But it's the add-ons that get you, and I had now assumed the costs. My daughter kept her word about taking care of them, though, until she went away on a class trip and left me in possession of a very long set of instructions.

CHICKEN TO-DO LIST

MORNING:

1. When you get up, check the chicks' general appearance first. They should be bright, lively, and sleeping together. If one is off by itself, tap the box near it and look in. If it moves and appears all right, move on.

2. Check the water. If empty, refer to the instructions on filling. Check feed. If empty or running low, especially if you're going out, add food. If everything else seems okay, move on.

AFTERNOON:
1. Perform same check as morning. Follow feed and water steps as needed.
2. Take out three to six chickens, either individually or two at a time. Make sure no predators are in the room at the time of removal.

BEFORE BED:
1. Perform morning check.
2. Fill out daily log entry.

NIGHT:
There is no need to check chickens during the night, except for the following reasons.

1. If a chicken is sick or injured, refer to the sickness or injury section, then perform five or more nightly checks.
2. If a chicken has died, check the other birds three or more times during the night to make sure there was no epidemic.

3. If you have made a large change in the chickens' light, heat, surroundings, feed, water, or bedding, check one to three times, depending on the change.

SICKNESS OR INJURY:

If a chicken shows signs of being sick or injured, pick it up carefully if the situation allows, and examine it.

- Its eyes should be bright. Are they caked shut or clouded?
- Its feathers should be normal-looking. Are they dull or bloodied?
- Its feet, legs, and wings should bend and flex gently with no pain to the bird.
- Its crop, the area on its breast, between the keel bone and neck, should be soft but not watery, not too full, and not hard or grainy.

If this check shows nothing alarming, replace the chick in the brooder and keep an eye on it. If a chicken becomes sick or injured, please refer to *Storey's Guide to Raising Chickens*. This should give you adequate information on what to do. Then call me if it gets serious. The latter step is very important.

DEATH:

1. If a chick dies, remove it quickly from the brooder so that the other chicks don't eat it.

2. Try to determine cause of death.
3. Dispose of it.
4. Disinfect waterer and feeder and clean cage.
5. Monitor other chicks for sickness.

HAVE FUN!

The day of her departure, she made me promise to disinfect their feeder. I went to the dump twice in a torrential rain, changed my soaking clothes, had tea and a croissant, started the dishwasher, and cleared my desk. When I could procrastinate no longer, I went to work. First, because this is just how I am, I organized the entire library for chicken chores. I swept. I moved the refrigerator box so that the passage around it was wider. Around the edges of the room I carefully arranged the bags of wood chips, rolls of paper towels, chicken-related literature, and spray bottles of the ever-important peroxide and vinegar. I cleaned up the bathroom where they had previously been housed. The brooder was still in the bathtub full of old bedding. Wood chips and chicken food were everywhere. I swept. I used liberal amounts of bleach. I taped the six pages of instructions to the library door, kept closed to keep out predators. I disinfected the feeder. I had never done it before. It went well.

I ran into trouble when I reached the afternoon checklist, namely "take out three to six chickens, either individually or two at a time. Make sure no predators are in the room." It had been a few days since I had handled the chicks and they were not used to me. I was in and out of their room, but I had put the access door to the box at ground level, which made my visitations difficult. I could once sit on the floor cross-legged and rise smoothly into a standing position without using my hands, but those days had long since passed, and now my descent to and ascent from the floor was neither quick, graceful, nor pain-free. As a result, I held the chicks when my daughter fetched them out, but I did not do the catching. And now, when I tried to take them out for their spin around the room, they would not let me near them. One of them, Brownie, who my daughter thought was a rooster and I thought might be a hawk, came over and pecked at my fingers, which didn't hurt but offended me just the same. And all of them panicked and fluttered to the far corner of the box when I tried to touch them.

Let me say that I was stung by their rejection. It was a poor time for them to spurn me. They looked like hell. Their feathers were coming in as quills and they looked like porcupines crossed with dust balls. Their combs had emerged lower on their foreheads than one might have wished, and bisected their heads to the crown. It was not an attractive look. But my daughter would be gone for three days, and I feared that due to my failure the chickens would grow wild. Because I did not want them to reject my daughter when she returned, I turned to the wise ones, the chicken masters of Backyard Chickens.

Suggestions included herding them into a corner with a flyswatter, scooping rather than grabbing (mother hens scoop, predators grab), climbing into the box to get them, and bribing them with worms. I herded them into a corner of the box with the old brooder lid and managed to scoop rather than grab three of them. I felt only half successful. I had gotten them out, but I had succeeded only in making them more leery of me.

While my daughter was away she called me every night.

"Are the chickens okay?"

"They are."

"Would you tell me if they weren't?"

"I would."

This last was a complete lie, and the only correct answer. It reminded me of the old joke about the two brothers. One goes away and leaves his beloved cat with the other. The first day, the cat dies. But the brother decides to break the news slowly. Every night his brother calls.

"How is the cat?"

"The cat is on the roof and it won't come down."

"How is the cat?" asks the brother the next night.

"He's still on the roof and he is getting weaker. We are very worried about him."

"How is the cat?" asks the brother on the third night.

"I'm sorry to tell you this, but the cat died."

The brother was bereft. Then he asked, "So, how's Mom?"

"Mom's on the roof," said his brother, "and she won't come down."

My daughter returned from her class trip, said hello to me, and ran in to see the chickens. She sat on the floor, opened the door of the pen, and the chickens, every last one of them, by God, strolled right out of that box and perched all over her.

The Ark

Meanwhile, spring had brought with it more than just chickens. It brought the blossoming of every tree, shrub, and flower on our beautiful hill. In the early days of our time in this house, it sat exposed on a barren hillside at the confluence of two roads until my husband became obsessed with planting. Large shipments of winterberry and holly, arrowwood viburnum, low bush blueberries, and fly honeysuckle arrived in our driveway regularly. Vermont forsythia, magnolia, rose of Sharon, rhododendron, and mountain laurel joined them in our now heavily populated yard. After all the years in our house, and after the deterioration of our marriage, that spring the yard was finally completed. The clematis he had given me years before on Mother's Day had grown like a weed and wound itself all over the front porch. We were leaving.

In one week I signed two purchase and sale agreements, one for the house I was selling and one for the house I was buying. I did well. I always did well. I stepped up to the plate. I took care of business. I did what had to be done. I had an optimism, a faith in the world as beautiful, that seemed to be hardwired into my being, unaffected by circumstance. I had friends and family, a good house, and money enough for a while. And I was relieved; the thing was done. But now I sat in my office in Hearts-Are-Cold, looking out the window at the yard, and cried for five days. On weekends I drove to Connecticut to visit my father in the hospital. I swore to Sage that I couldn't do this. I talked with Penny so many times a day that I began to hate her telephone numbers.

The library remained full of chickens, chicken abodes, and chicken paraphernalia. A bucket of grain, a bag of grit, a giant paper parcel of pine shavings, three trash bags, a water bucket, assorted chairs, *Storey's Guide to Raising Chickens*, and two or three partially used rolls of paper towels. The chickens continued their busy, contented chicken lives, eating, drinking, fussing over minutia, and laying around listening to classical music. They were starting to smell. The refrigerator box was on its last legs. It was time for the babies to graduate.

There are about a billion variables that go into properly securing space for poultry. Most important, the chickens needed a coop and a yard into which my dog and other animals would not be able to dig, climb, or jump. I spent some time perusing the Backyard Chicken archives, and I was dismayed to learn that I had to worry not only about my dog, but about everyone else's dogs, as well as cats, raccoons, foxes, coyotes, owls, hawks, fisher cats, mink, bobcats, mountain lions, bears, gators, wolverines, and panthers. Because I lived in eastern Massachusetts, I considered deleting gators and wolverines from my list of worries.

By then, as an established member of the Backyard Chicken community, I had read many things. I knew that if my dog killed a chicken I was to tie the dead chicken around her neck until it rotted, though there were those who swore this was no deterrent at all. I knew that if I trapped a predator, I was to throw the varmint-filled trap into the creek for ten minutes, thus eliminating the possibility of its return. I knew about chicken wire, floodlights, and that having a male human pee around the perimeter of my yard was supposed to deter unwanted nocturnal visitors. One thread on the predator section of the message board ran six pages and had 121 posts. The topic was coyotes. The messages ranged from methods of trapping to extended philosophical debates on predator control. Contributors to this conversation ranged from grizzled backwoodsmen to teenage girls who objected to killing of any kind, ever, for any reason, and who wrote their messages in gigantic bright pink or fluorescent turquoise typefaces.

I was terrified about predators. Backyard Chickens was not enough. I needed the wisdom of local chicken owners.

· · ·

I suspected, but was not sure, that there were chickens hidden all over Hearts-Are-Cold. I had seen suspicious-looking sheds here and there, and the animal clinic had a sign on the counter offering "Fresh Eggs, $2 a dozen." My first post-chicken visit to the vet, to have my dog's nails trimmed, gave me the opportunity to enquire about their chicken coop security measures.

The animal clinic, with its small, dirty waiting area and two run-down examining rooms, had seen better days. The vets came and went, but the three women who ran the place remained constant. These women were unconcerned with shades of lipstick or the decision whether to use cream or powdered eye shadow. They appeared to be oblivious to the condition of their hair, which was long and gray and unruly. They dressed without regard to fashion, in jeans and men's shirts. I admired them terribly and felt terribly inferior to them. At the desk on the day in question sat a large woman with long unkempt gray hair and a gruff voice. She wore an old blue flannel shirt over what looked like a man's ripped undershirt. I had never seen her smile. I sat my dog down on the dirty floor, and in what felt like a very wimpy voice I asked for her advice on building a chicken coop.

"Don't make it too big," she growled. "And make it raccoon-proof."

"Oh," said I. "You've had problems with raccoons?" I knew that raccoons were a serious predator of chickens, I knew how they ate them and what they left behind. But I didn't look like I knew that.

"They come," she said. "But they don't leave."

I could see where this was going. "You . . . shoot them," I said. Nonchalant. Matter-of-fact. Cool. She nodded.

"With a twenty-two," she said, looking at me out of the corner of her eye.

I thought I was doing a pretty good job of holding my own considering that I was wearing a new lime-green T-shirt, black cropped pants, and very expensive shoes. I nodded sagely, like a woman who had a .22 leaning up against her own bedroom door and knew how the hell to use it. I went home wondering what, exactly, a .22 looked like, where to get one, and whether I would ever be able to shoot well enough to hit a raccoon at two A.M. in bare feet and pajamas. I imagined myself macing a savage coyote and wondered about my worthiness as a poultry farmer.

We had an old shed on our property, one side filled with tools and old cans of motor oil and half-used-up paint, the other filled with lawn chairs, sleds, inner tubes, and the last vestiges of my daughter's playhouse, the Apothecary, a throwback to Harry Potter days, that had once been stocked with dried roots and a dog-eared copy of *A Field Guide to Medicinal Plants*. The tool side had a dirt floor and broken windows and no ceiling. The Apothecary had a wooden floor, intact windows with functional shutters, half of a ceiling, and a door that was stuck shut. It was starting to look good for the coop.

The day came when I put on my not-as-expensive-shoes, opened my rudimentary toolbox, and selected my weapons. Armed with stiff new leather work gloves, hardware cloth, a hammer, nails, and my newly purchased fifteen-inch tin snips, I bravely walked out into the summer day. I kicked open the shed door and gave it a good look. Looked up, looked down, looked to the sides, and the vestigial engineer in me saw right away that it couldn't be done. I was stunned. I walked inside and put away my stuff.

The following day I did it again, not because I was wrong the first time, but because in the interim I'd convinced myself that it could, in fact, work. Got the tools. Kicked open the door. It couldn't be done. Next day, same thing. Then I told everyone I knew not to let me go out there again.

And so I set out to buy a doghouse at a distant unfinished-furniture store. They told me they had huge doghouses, three by four feet, plenty big enough for the transitional coop. This had been done before; I had seen it on Backyard Chickens. An hour of stop-and-go traffic later—a truck carrying a load of snow crabs had overturned and spilled its cargo all over Route 3—I pulled into the parking lot to find a tiny doghouse. I stared at it with a sinking heart.

"Whadaya thinkin'?" the guy asked me. "Tell me what ya thinkin'."

"I'm thinkin' it's too small," I said.

I studied it. It was definitely too small. But then I spied another thing, something called a trash shed that had hinged doors and was the right size. I had a nice conversation with the cashier, whose grandfather had bought her chickens and goats that swam in the pool and had to be pulled out by her father before they drowned.

I had my coop. As for the rest, there are two basic choices with chickens. They free-range—putter around unfettered and unconfined—or they putter around within the confines of a fence, also known as a run. We needed one. Foxes regularly and ostentatiously trotted across our patio day and night. A run can be slightly less impenetrable than a coop because most chicken predators are nocturnal, or crepuscular, prowling at dawn and dusk when the chickens are safely in bed. But the top of the run needed to be covered. Chickens can fly. Bantams can fly over seven feet high, and the heavier breeds can fly about four feet. The longest chicken flight ever recorded lasted seventeen seconds, which doesn't seem so long until you count it, one Mississippi, two Mississippi, and imagine that it is a chicken you are watching fly, not a blue jay or a crow.

The enclosed run should include ten square feet per bird, for which we had plenty of room, but the need for flat, boulder-free ground eliminated much of our yard from consideration. Then, in my Internet voyages, I discovered something called an ark, a triangular run covered with chicken wire. I questioned the wisdom of it. I wondered why not a *rectangular* structure covered with chicken wire.

"The triangle is the most stable shape on earth," my daughter told me, and I was not going to argue with her. A triangle it would be. She printed out eighteen pages of ark pictures.

"They don't look so hard to make," I said.

"No," she said. "They don't."

"We could do that," I said.

"I think we could," she said, thus making what would be her last contribution to our first chicken coop.

Building the ark took Noah a while, I suppose. My ark took me four days. I spent much of the four days thinking. I sat on the ground and stared into the distance for long periods of time. My nights were disturbed with new ideas and worries. How would I build a door? How would I fit the rectangular coop onto the triangular ark? Why did I think I could do this?

I had never built anything before. I was working with primitive tools. I needed a table saw, an electric miter saw, and sawhorses. Instead, I had a dull handsaw, a right angle, and a pair of green plastic lawn chairs. I had fifty feet of chicken wire rolled out on my driveway. Unlike hardware cloth, which, once you cut it, pretty much stays in the shape you want, chicken wire is an unruly foe. Tin snips hack right through hardware cloth. Cutting chicken wire with tin snips is like cutting paper with the scissors in your left hand.

The run would be ten feet long, six feet wide at the base, and five feet high at the peak of the triangle. On the first day I built two rectangular frames for the sides of the triangle and covered them with chicken wire. On the second day I built the door frame and the door. I drilled holes along the top of the side frames and attached them together with zip ties. Now I had a standing triangle. On the third day I made a window for the little coop and drilled ventilation holes. I dragged the triangle into the backyard—a staggering feat— and covered the open end with chicken wire. I spent several hours sitting on a rock trying to figure out how to attach the other end of the ark to the coop. It couldn't be done, really, but I was driven by a steely desperation and so I did it anyway.

I took prophylactic Motrin every night. I hammered, sta- pled, cut, and measured. I mitered. I sweat, bled, and used most of the profanity I knew, loudly. I talked to myself. I had no Band-Aids. I looked at the run, thought about it, gave up several times, and cried. On the evening of the third day, I went directly from my carpentry to pick my daughter up at her friend's house, a huge house in Hearts-Are-Cold, and I believe that when I rang the bell some of the guests at the cocktail party thought I was an employee. On the morning of the fourth day, I hung the door on its hinges, attached a handle, and then my daughter and I added the chickens. They were now where they were supposed to be: outside, in the grass, in the sun, under the trees, in the breeze. They flapped and hopped and jumped on each other. They caught worms and ran around with them. They sat on the roost. They ate, drank, and slept. Free at last, more or less, and the dog slept, exhausted and for once uninterested, in a sunny patch of dust.

I questioned many times in those four days why I had consented to this madness, these chickens, this labor. It would be several months before I would realize that these chickens were a bridge. The logistics of moving, the yard, the legal documents, Penny and her perfume, these were temporary. The chickens were the thread, the real thing that pulled us, stumbling and fearful, into the future.

And as for me, I recovered. I spent part of the third night in the emergency room with an accelerated heart rate, a benign malady, sometimes stress-induced, that occasionally required me to make a middle-of-the-night voyage to the hospital. I took a cab home at four thirty A.M. The sky was lightening over the harbor. I wondered why I didn't get up that early every morning. It was beautiful and quiet and gray, and the water and the sky were exactly the same color. I got home and went to bed, slept for five hours, and finished the run. I had never built anything before, and then, like Noah, I built an ark. When I look at pictures of it now, it doesn't seem that complicated, but, like the seventeen-second flight of the chicken, it does when I think about it.

Guardians

To my daughter a gray house was just one step up from a brown house and therefore only narrowly escaped condemnation. "Paint it white," she told me, and she was not happy when I said that I wouldn't. That the house had vinyl siding only increased her disdain. As for me, I would never tire of driving down the bumpy roads of my new neighborhood, past the asphalt-shingled houses and the squat brick houses, and coming around the corner to that little gray house. The trees on the south side of the house were in leaf, as was the ragged front hedge. The big lawn was green. The pond was blue. From a certain spot on the yard I could see the ocean. Inside the kitchen, if the tiny opaque window was open, and if I stood on my tiptoes, I could see a very thin line of blue.

The house had many visitors that summer. My mother came to help me pack and brought along my older brother, fresh from his own separation and in need of a distraction. What the chickens were for my daughter, I would be for my brother, at least for a weekend. His mind worked in quiet ways, but he was a person who could do anything, it seemed: build a chimney, a house, a pitching machine for his son. His business card was made of two small pieces of wood, one light, one dark, so intricately put together that no one could figure out how he did it. While my mother took hold of the kitchen, rolling everything into paper and carefully boxing it, my brother took my dog for long walks and fixed three electrical cords she had chewed through when she was a puppy. He walked around the new house and yard, seeing everything that would ever need to be done with it. That tree trimmed and that piece of window fixed, a tiny leak in a pipe plugged. I promptly forgot it all, only to remember it weeks or months later when it actually did need to be done.

My mother packed and cooked. She is a determined cook, and I had to remind myself that she enjoyed it, as I did not. My childhood seemed to have been whipped in butter and cream and brown sugar from her kitchen, and I was still addicted to cookies, unhappy with any but hers.

In the evenings, when we had finished packing for the day, we all sat at the big kitchen table, and my mother taught my daughter how to play poker. My brother slept on the couch in my office and swore in the mornings, as if I should have known, as if it was something that anyone would know, that he'd been kept awake all night by seagulls.

My father came, having survived the biopsy that almost killed him, moving on to battle the cancer that *would* eventually kill him. My father had clear gray eyes and a piercing and relentless intelligence. My parents were long divorced and my father had met the last love of his life at the age of seventy. He had raced cars until he was seventy-five. Now eighty, facing the end of his years, his courage would not fail him. He told me later that he feared the worst as I drove past the boxy cottages on the road that, by a strange quirk of fate, bore my husband's first name, but which my daughter and I called Dwiggins Path after a juvenile duck we found there one morning. But as we came around the bend to the little hidden spot tucked into the corner of the pond and sheltered by the wooded peninsula beyond, my father breathed again.

"Now I know you're going to be all right," he said. We drove to the beach and sat a while in the car, next to an ancient Silver Cloud, against which leaned an impossibly aged chauffeur in an equally antique uniform, reading a newspaper. A tough guy with a pit bull on a leash walked by and turned in a double take. "Holy s——," he said with wonder. "That's a Rolls-Royce."

Friends came to survey the new house. They peered into the milky windows and examined the yard. The Moon

Women sat on the broken benches of the peeling red picnic table on the mildewed deck and ate the salads that Sage had brought from a deli near her house. They looked at the kitchen through the windows of the sliding doors.

"What's that in the middle of it?" asked Martha.

"It's a wall," said Sage.

"That kitchen looks perfectly fine to me," said Scarlet, who was game for anything.

And what seemed like an endless procession of workmen came, to look, to measure, to estimate, to say whether it could or could not be done. Some I knew from Hearts-Are-Cold. Some were new. Some would become surrogate brothers or fathers or husbands for the many months it would take me to finish the first layer of renovations. They would see me through, those men. They would be there for me, would come on the first day of their vacations, on Saturdays, in emergencies, and on time. They would become my family.

No one tried to talk me out of what I knew they thought was a project of relatively insane proportions. No one told me it was a bad idea. But I knew they thought it, and I was afraid. This was no home; it was no refuge. It was a visage, a daydream, wishful thinking. It was a collection of Herculean labors. An empty gray house. My daughter, usually one to wear her emotions wildly, was disturbingly quiet, and I suffered in her pale silence. Against all of her instincts for self-preservation, she withheld her riotous, willful disapproval because she trusted me. She refused all of my encouragements to enter the new house, however, save one, and then she walked quickly through the empty rooms and out the front door.

"I'm ready to go," she said.

In Hearts-Are-Cold, I hired Pete from the hardware store to clean out the basement and the shed while I started packing the bedrooms. In my daughter's room, I was helpless. She had inherited the don't-throw-anything-away gene from her father, and her room was a compendium of interests long since abandoned. Straw flowers on wire stems from a second-grade art project. A Snoopy suitcase stuffed with unrecognizable white pottery. Precariously balanced baskets of Super Balls with pods of killer whales or dolphins or penguins floating in them, squashed pennies from penny-squashing machines, tiny containers containing nothing, hundreds of homemade beads, gooey rubber insects, worms that stuck to walls, jars of fairy dust, dozens of key rings, and a small ceramic seal designed to be a holder for gum that one had already chewed but might want to chew again later.

Intermingled with all of this were the Guardians. For

three years, starting when she was eight, my daughter made small creatures out of polymer clay, gave them hardware appendages, and baked them. The Guardians started out simple—a body, maybe screws for legs, and beads for eyes— but became exponentially more complicated.

They were not cute. Any Guardian that featured a piece of hardware with a pointed end had that pointed end aiming outward. A typical Guardian might have a foot-long chain-link tail ending in multiple nail-studded balls. Or spikes emerging from its forehead and spine. Or construction staple teeth tipped with nail-polish blood. Dozens of small round Guardians with beady eyes hung by their sharp metal tails from a wire strung above my daughter's bed. There were thousands of Guardians. There were warrior Guardians, worker Guardians, merchant Guardians, and feeder Guardians. There were footed, winged, and finned Guardians. None of them was cute.

My daughter's art teacher once told me, "She isn't afraid of ugliness." And indeed, the Guardians represented the moment in my parenthood when I finally knew that I did not understand at all the depth of my daughter's bold and fearless mind. At first I wondered what people would think about her and her fierce creations. And people did, I could tell, have thoughts about the Guardians, and presumably their maker and her mother as well. Get over it, I told myself. And over time, I did. I came to appreciate their wildness and their complex personalities and their intricate social and military structure. I didn't care what people thought. I assessed a person's creativity by their degree of interest in, and lack of horror at, the Guardians.

In time, the Guardians assumed control of my daughter's imagination, her creativity, her free time, and most of our house. She had several plastic storage cases with drawers and compartments full of clay, nails, screws, prongs, chains, and springs. We became habitués of the hardware store, where we spent so much time that the owner told my daughter he'd hire her as soon as she turned fifteen.

Three years after their advent, the Guardians stopped cold and she never looked back. But her room was littered with them, and, as I packed, I mourned their passing and the passing of all the other discarded things of her childhood. I made impossible decisions about what to keep and what to let go. My daughter, who I had promised I would involve in the decision about where to move, and to whom in the end I had only said, "You have to trust me on this one," and who did. My precociously brilliant and fierce only child, whose huge imagination I had only ever seen challenged once, by this move. Who, when her school project was to decorate a small box in honor of her hero, chose me. Who once drew a picture of her own head with a large hawk, wings spread, behind it. "It's her mind," her teacher said.

She was changing that summer, as if overnight, from

someone who made elaborate movies featuring her friends in homemade costumes and rubber elf ears, and llamas made of cardboard covered with fake fur. She was becoming a young teenager interested in makeup, mud masques, alternative rock, and boys. She put her hands on her hips and said things like, "You can't do that," and "Why *can't* I do that," and "You just don't understand," and "I want to be alone." The first time, I thought she was kidding. Then she got even madder and I realized that, after almost thirteen years, my reign as a person who could do no wrong was coming to an end. She had one foot in childhood and one foot in something I hadn't yet caught up with. She was only twelve, with a twelve-year-old's body, attitude, and hormones, but she had the mind of a judge and the soul of a Druid priestess.

We were moving five minutes away. We would go to the same library, the same hardware store, the same supermarket, and the same convenience store when we ran out of milk for cereal. She would have the same school and the same friends. We would go to the same beach, the same movie theaters, and the same drugstore. But moving her from the house she loved was the hardest thing I ever did.

In June she gathered her collection of bones and shells and horseshoe crabs.

"I'm going to put them back, now," she said, and took them down to the cove. When she returned she told me that she had placed the bleached-white seagull skull in the water facing the island on which the seagulls built their nests every summer and raised their gawky chicks.

Nothing would be as hard as that.

My heart broke so many times that summer that I lost count of when or why. At night I lay awake and mentally revised my lists and calendars. I obsessively cut pages out of decorating and gardening magazines and pasted them into a large bound sketchbook that quickly bulged at the seams. "Have a vision," one article urged, "and don't lose sight of it." I did have a vision and I never would lose sight of it. But there were days when that vision was cold comfort, promising only a new shell in which to live. The price for what I was leaving—the old skins of my marriage and house—was fear.

After my daughter's room, I became ruthless. I graduated from Pete and his pickup to Ed Crowe, who came equipped with a really, *really* big truck, a hydraulic lift, and a saws-all. Ed was a short, stocky man with a huge stomach. He was possessed of brute strength and a willingness to dismantle and remove almost anything, red-faced, dripping sweat, and dispensing landscaping advice as he went. By the end, Ed would have taken away six huge truckloads of miscellaneous stuff from both of my houses. My houses would be like the little cars in the circus from which too many clowns emerged. They would be like the sleeves of the Banana Man from which appeared more bananas and scarves than were possible, accompanied by even the Banana Man's own surprised squeals.

July whirled past. All of my plans kicked into action. I had the floors sanded and stained, the bathroom redone, the moldering deck power-washed, and I didn't even *own* the house yet. People helped me. They fit me in. They moved me up on their lists. They did things they said they couldn't do. Workers showed up on time and left on time. I didn't know then how unusual that was, how lucky I was. I learned as I went that people wanted to help me, and that if I asked, if I explained, they did. And everything I asked, I asked for my daughter. The workmen sanded and finished, they tiled and sealed, tore out the wall in the middle of the kitchen and the weird counter in the corner, leaving a scar in the middle of the floor and a wall covered with thick brown glue. The chandelier came out, leaving two bare lightbulbs hanging from wires. The rusty stove left, leaving none. Dwiggins, the duck my daughter and I discovered in the straggly yews at the front of the house, who liked to hide in the bushes under the deck, got scared and ran away, never to be seen again.

My friend Sage and I cleaned what we could. We scrubbed and mopped and washed and disinfected. Then we did it again and again. The kitchen floor alone took about ten passes. We went through two mops, several sponges, and canisters of disinfectant wipes. We went through buckets of filthy water. We broke one mop right in half. When we were finished with the downstairs, we tackled the attic rooms. After about five minutes I had the feeling that although we seemed to be cleaning, we really weren't, and that the rooms would be dirty forever.

I wore my cell phone clipped to my waistband. I wrote checks at every turn. I borrowed money from my mother, my ex-husband, and my retirement account. When my house sold, a big chunk of my earnings would repay these debts. The rest would continue to reinvent this good little house.

A week before moving day, I became obsessed with the kitchen floor, the peeling linoleum, the hole in the middle of it where the wall had been, the fact that it looked so unwashable that I wasn't sure I would be able to walk on it barefoot, and decided to rip it up and install a new one before we moved. I would live without a stove, sink, or refrigerator for the six weeks it would take to get the new kitchen cabinets if I could just have that floor. I had ordered neither the flooring nor the cabinets. The floor guy looked at me like I was nuts.

"You can't do that," he said.

"I have to."

"You can't," he repeated. "*I* can't."

So I folded up cardboard boxes and duct-taped them into

the nine-foot-long, six-inch-wide, two-inch-deep scar left by the wall. I would get used to that kitchen, the naked bulbs and the scarred floor, the cardboard and the duct tape, the peeling Formica, the unusable cupboards, the tiny opaque window, and the gummy brown wall. I would get *comfortable* in that kitchen. That kitchen would get *homey*. The real problem was not living in squalor. The real problem was that you can get used to anything.

What I Left Behind

Here is where I stood. There was no electricity. There was no toilet and no bathroom sink. There was no chicken coop. All of this had to happen between dawn and noon on moving day. I left for Six Mile Beach at seven A.M. to meet the electricians, the plumber, the handyman, and the men who would build the shed for the chickens. I felt good about the plumber and the handyman and the electricians. I was worried about the shed. But the men arrived on time, and put together a six-by-eight-foot coop with a perfect latch on the door and windows that swung inward and came with locks already attached. I adored them for it. I thought they might have run over the sewer pipes, but they weren't worried. They gestured at the huge truck.

"It doesn't weigh much," they said.

They were cheerful and kind and added nothing to the weight on my shoulders. They did their job and waved good-bye. The fence men, two brothers trading insults, attached a run to the shed, the electricians began redoing the electrical services, and the handyman went to work on the basement. The plumber discovered that the new sink was broken to bits in its box. We would spend the first night in our house without one.

I returned to Hearts-Are-Cold. I hadn't hired the good movers because I was trying to save money. Now, meeting my discount movers at the door, I realized my error. They arrived on time, but I knew right away that I had to worry about them, that they would do their job, but barely, and that I had no chance on earth of making it through the day with any semblance of peace. No one was in charge but me. They commenced moving, but they seemed to be doing it very slowly. My nerve endings frayed, operating on full alert, I turned to the next thing I could do. I mustered my forces and prepared to move the chickens.

It seemed like a good idea to move the chickens in a dog crate, so I set it up next to the ark. I stood ready. My daughter caught the chickens one at a time. As soon as each chicken went in, it tried to get out, and because the chickens were faster than my ability to slam the crate door without inflicting injury or decapitation, they succeeded. Chicken One went in. Chicken Two went in and Chicken One got out. Chicken One went back in. Chicken Three went in and Chicken Two got out. Back in with Chicken Two, out with Chicken Three.

My daughter stood before me holding Chicken Four.

"This isn't going to work," I said. I got a packing box and punched holes in it with a pair of scissors. Chickens Four, Five, and Six descended into the box without a hitch. It was ten o'clock. My husband and daughter drove the dog and the six chickens over to Six Mile Beach while I stayed behind in Hearts-Are-Cold to dismantle my beautiful ark.

Chicken wire is like a wild animal, safe only when confined. Released from its staples and roofing nails and its frame of timbers, it ran rampant over my efforts to tame it. The new owners arrived to approve the house's condition before the closing. They were tidy, well dressed, and expressionless. I was bleeding profusely from a scratch on my forehead. I wiped the blood off on my T-shirt. I pointed to the clematis on the front-stair railing and told them that they shouldn't cut it back in the winter. I said they should have the trees trimmed every year. The woman nodded primly and said nothing. Then I went back to the coop while they toured the house and became the second big thing that went wrong with my day.

They were upset that I was still in the process of moving out. They were upset because the house was old and their insurance agent had told them that they had a month to fix the many things needing fixing. I had vacuumed the whole house, cleaned the kitchen, and scrubbed the bathrooms. But they had never bought a house before. They had lived overseas, in houses that were provided them by his business, and were, no doubt, pristine in comparison to mine.

Now they had bought an old house that, when dolled up for open houses, full of fresh flowers and primroses, looked really good. But my house in mid-move was not a pretty sight. Where furniture used to be were now coins and pens and chew toys rolled in dust. While I was busy scratching myself on chicken wire, they almost walked away from the sale. Penny promised them house cleaners, landscapers, trash services, and new insurance brokers. She made the phone calls and set it all up. She soothed and smoothed over. Penny was all about inspiring trust. She said all along that she put people first and it turned out that she meant it. When she had changed agencies in the middle of selling my house, and was told that she would not get a commission, she told me she would not abandon me during the sale. And then she pulled a billion rabbits out of her fashionable hat to save it.

But although it would go through, the sale of the house had taken on a sour feeling. The new owners barely spoke to me at the closing. I was not well enough dressed to sell my house in Hearts-Are-Cold, but they were well enough dressed to buy it. The dress I had planned to wear, the dress I had carefully draped over the back of a kitchen chair that very morning, had disappeared hours ago. I went to the closings in the clothes I had started the day in: baggy shorts and T-shirt and sneakers without socks. I went dirty. I went with my daughter and my dog. At the other closing, in which I

bought the gray house in Six Mile Beach, Mr. G.—the seller
and my soon-to-be next-door neighbor—attended with his
entire extended family and joked in his heavily accented En-
glish about having to get more chickens in order to catch up,
my six to his five, and no one cared how I looked. Weeks
later, on a camping trip, I found the dress rolled into a ball on
the floor of my car. I also found a screwdriver, a hammer,
three construction-grade protective face masks, wire cutters
and a small roll of hardware cloth, the dog's Invisible Fence
collar, several half-full water bottles, a box of crackers, a
chisel, two and a half pairs of shoes, and a box of nails. I
could have built a small shelter and lived for a week on what
was in the back of that car. I could have started a construction company.

Between the two closings I received a call from one of the
movers. They were concerned because it looked like my
king-size bed frame was not going to fit down the stairs. I
had worried about that. My mother-in-law, bless her, had
once told me in her breathy, well-to-do voice, to "Run, don't
walk, to the nearest furniture store and buy a king-size bed."
And so I had. Now I remembered the call I had gotten when
the bed did not fit *up* the stairs.

"Take off the banister," I had told them. They did, and the
bed went up. Now it would not come down.

"Cut it in half," I told him.

"You're kidding," he said. I was not.

The movers, who had promised me they'd be done by noon, didn't finish until almost six. At three, I left my daughter in Six Mile Beach with a friend and returned to Hearts-Are-Cold to pick up whatever they had left behind. They had gotten the bed down after all, without cutting it in half, but they had left two or three carloads of miscellaneous belongings.

As I was stuffing my car with curtains and tools and left-over bags of cleaning supplies, the new owners arrived with floor sanders and paint, still neatly attired and expressionless. I could now decipher their expressionlessness as disapproval. They sat on the patio and talked on their cell phones—to their attorneys, I was sure—while I stacked final things in my car. I stood for a moment in each empty room, filled with echoes. I had not wanted to stay in this house when my husband and I separated. I had done so because it was best for my daughter, although, house-poor, we had only lasted a year. My husband had moved nearby, to a little cottage on the bank of a river, and I had cried whenever I saw it. I had so desperately wanted a new beginning. My house had seemed drab and full of used-up dreams.

I'd coped with staying by having big plans for the house,

most of which involved knocking out a huge number of walls, and none of which I could afford. I'd also planned, blithely overlooking my introverted nature, to have many large dinner parties and intellectually stimulating salons in which people would recite poetry and read aloud from interesting books. These things did not happen either, at least not in this version of the universe, but the rooms held a kind of shadow of those dinner parties, as if perhaps they had happened in a parallel one.

Now, as I stood in each empty room, I was surprised at the dullness of the floors, the scuffs on the baseboards, and the nail holes in the walls. I was surprised that I had never painted over the green woodwork in my office or replaced the ugly sliding doors in our bedroom. I was bone tired and in shock from the day. I took down curtains and checked that the closets were empty. The new owners followed me closely to make sure I left nothing behind, no stray pen or curtain rod. I didn't feel terrible; it would be weeks before I even knew that the things I left behind had nothing to do with possessions.

It was a house where the wind always blew across the front yard and the buoy bells my mother had given me always rang. The huge crab apple tree outside my office window exploded in pink every spring. Once my husband had tried and failed to string it with Christmas lights, and settled on a shrub instead, where the lights assumed their year-round home. My daughter had ridden her bicycle around and around the block, a circular loop dead-ending at the sanctuary, where all of the rangers knew her by name. "Going around again!" she'd shout on her way around. She checked the cove repeatedly in the spring for horseshoe crabs, and at low tide you could still see the tops of a pair of pink rubber boots sticking up out of the mud where she had gotten stuck when she was seven and I'd had to wade out to pull her from her permanently stuck boots and carry her to shore. At night, great horned owls called and answered, called and answered, and once, as I was looking out of the window of my dark bedroom, trying to see them, one flew by so fast and so silently, and so close to my window, that I fell over backward. My daughter and her friends did acrobatic tricks on the rope swing and my dog would grab the rope tail of the swing, lift off, and soar over the backyard. My nineteen-year-old cat had died in that house. You don't just leave a place and get away with all of yourself.

At six, I walked one last time through the empty rooms. Ed Crowe came and sawed down the wooden swing set. He dismantled my ark and carried it away in his big truck.

That evening, my daughter and I drove back to Hearts-Are-Cold for dinner at our old neighbors' house. I was wearing the same clothes I had worn all day because I didn't know where any of my other clothes were. Gunny, who raised four children in a house in which shoes were not allowed, did not bat an eyelash. She made my daughter's favorite crab dip. She made chicken and potatoes and salad. We ate on the deck where the breeze came in off the cove. I drank gallons of iced tea. I had not sat down in hours. Those moments felt like heaven.

It could have been worse, but not a whole lot. It didn't rain. The sales of the houses went through. Everything— animate and inanimate—left one house and ended up in the other. Other than that, it was a day I had nightmares about for weeks. I dreamt that I had built the shed at the wrong house. I dreamt that I had to dismantle a barn bolt by bolt. But that first night in my new house I did not dream. I lay sleepless on the living room couch with a regular phone, a cell phone, a flashlight, and a hammer. It was so quiet. It was quieter than anything. I looked out the window at the silent front yard and kept expecting something to happen, but nothing ever did.

In the Beginning

Our first week in the house the basement flooded twice, I dropped two hundred pounds of drywall on my leg, and so many workmen came that my daughter begged me to make them leave. The handyman, the electricians, the plumber, the fence builders, the chimney sweep: They were our constant companions. The floods were taken care of by the Six Mile Beach Water Department because they were the ones who had turned off the pump in the year that my house had been empty. They drained the basement with two gigantic hoses and dried it with seven enormous fans. A week later, a deluge hit town, dumping two inches of rain in an hour, most of which poured down the walls of my basement. Just then, the guys showed up to collect the fans, brought out the hoses again, and sucked the water out. The house would buzz with fans for another week, in which time my leg, miraculously unbroken, turned purple and swelled to twice its normal size. But it did not hurt, because most of the nerves in the front of my leg had been crushed, and so I was able to carry on.

"Can you spend an hour every afternoon with your leg

up?" asked my doctor. I didn't think so. The leg would remain swollen and numb for a long, long time.

"Is this normal?" I would ask.

"I'm afraid so," the doctor would say, and say again the next time, and the next, until I stopped asking.

So I carried on. It was a year of carrying on.

My mother came and took over my berth on the couch. She bossed us around while I organized the basement and one of the upstairs rooms. She was there after the first flood, when the giant fans were still humming, and she was there for the second flood when the water poured down the walls of the basement and I cried privately, under the basement staircase. Rick, the electrician, showed up just after the big trucks left. The rain had stopped by then and the sun came out and we sat on the front steps as I told him what had happened. And I could tell he felt a little sorry for me and wondered if I regretted what I had done, buying this little mess of a house, but I didn't, and I never would.

The weather rolled in off the sea, and across the pond, and landed at our doorstep. It was cold at night, the air chilled by fog and mist. We slept under down comforters, but during the day, when it was warm, we left the windows open, and the doors, although they had no screens. Sometimes I thought that the house, for all it was in such terrible shape, and such a mess, would never again be as pure as it was then.

. . .

In the beginning, the living room was so full of furniture that we could barely get in. There was a hole in the bathroom wall with two large wires protruding from it. The upper walls of the bathroom were covered with partially stripped sea motif wallpaper. The kitchen was the kitchen, nothing different: hole in the floor, opaque window, crumbling counters. We lived without a stove, oven, or dishwasher. We had a hot plate, which didn't work very well, and I bought a countertop convection oven, which did. At first I loved washing dishes in the ancient sink, my arms in the warm soapy water, looking out the tiny window at the pond.

"I've decided not to get a dishwasher when I redo the kitchen," I told Sage one night as I sat, wounded leg up, the phone emitting bursts of static that the wiremen had not yet been able to fix.

"Well, maybe just get one," she said gently. "You don't have to use it." Life was immediate in those days, whittled down to basics, all the doors and windows thrown open. My rapture with washing dishes lasted for about a week.

I had amassed dozens of pictures of kitchens torn out of decorating magazines. Now I studied them. My daughter, who read *Fine Cooking* magazine for pleasure, and knew how to sear and deglaze and make a roux, wanted a kitchen of dark cherrywood and granite. She accompanied me to the upscale home improvement store, where we wandered through model kitchen after model kitchen. She kept a running commentary in which she analyzed the pros and cons of each, in language one might use to describe wine. She knew I was going to choose a kitchen with white cabinets and black counters and that the counters would not be granite, not even soapstone. She swore she would seal the soapstone once a month, and waxed poetic on the richness of granite, but it was my kitchen after all, and the counters and cabinets were the only things I knew for sure about it. Otherwise, I was stymied.

The Moon Women sat at the table in the makeshift kitchen one night in September and jolted me out of my paralytic state.

"I'm moving, too," said Scarlet. This came as a surprise since she had been in her tiny attic apartment only two years since her divorce.

"Tell me you are not moving to Texas," I said.

"Just around the corner," she assured me. "The guy who sold me my place is going to buy it back and sell me a new one. He's setting up the whole thing, mortgage and all. I can move in any time." She went on. Stainless steel appliances! Granite counters! Air-conditioning! Ceiling fans!

"The only thing I don't like is the carpets," she said. "So I told him to take them up and put down hardwood floors."

"He's going to do that?"

"Oh yes," she said serenely. He was also, inexplicably, taking care of all the legal work, the inspections, the mortgages, and the closing dates.

I had the electricians on Tuesday, the window guy on Wednesday, and the handyman on Thursday to put up the screen doors. I was picking up floor samples on Friday, and confirming cabinet measurements the following week. Somewhere in the recent past were floor sanding, tiling, painting, locksmithing, and plumbing. Somewhere in the near future lurked kitchen demolition, wall patching, full kitchen renovation, and landscaping. Scarlet, on the other hand, had a brand-new, fully refurbished apartment, with hardwood floors and stainless steel appliances and someone else had done it all, had taken care of everything, legal, financial, and practical. I was speechless with self-pity.

"Great!" I said, and, "I can't believe it!" And I really tried to mean it.

Spurred on by envy, I showed them my collection of kitchen pictures.

"This one," they pointed.

I ordered the cabinets the next day.

In the beginning we could not believe where we had landed. If you had told us that such a place existed we would have begged to differ. From a distance the hills of Six Mile Beach looked like a rustic and overcrowded Italian hill village. Closer up, at the corner of our street, brightly colored laundry hung on a line strung between two houses. And at our house, tucked in down by the corner of the pond, at the end of the path, were the Bindles, Phoebe, and the G.'s.

The G.'s were old, small, Italian, and sharp as tacks. Both had rich accents and glowed with intelligence. She brought me tomatoes and basil. Mr. G., or Jimmy the Barber, as he told me to call him, was in his late seventies and trimmed his hedges rigorously and bare-chested. "He was a barber," said Mrs. G. "Everything has to have a flattop." Which explained the severely trimmed yews in front of my house.

Mr. G. sold Dragonfly Farm to me when it was a cold, empty house with a wall in the middle of the kitchen, and he had chickens, five of them, in the wilderness between his house and the gravel pit. I visited once, in the summer, before I moved, and saw one chicken and many, many white rabbits, all of them in hutches, except for one, an apparent escapee. Mrs. G. told me that she wouldn't eat anything that came from "back there," but someone told me that white rabbits were the eating kind. Because of the rabbits there was a magical, otherworldly quality to their hidden farm. I felt transported to a magician's garden, in Italy, fifty years ago, where the muscadine vines grew wild behind the villa.

People seemed to give Mr. and Mrs. G. animals. Someone gave them a dovecote once, and fifty doves.

"The coyotes got them," said Mr. G.

"We had pigs once," said Mrs. G., "but best were the sheep."

They had sheep back there?

"Someone gave them," she said, and nodded as if it were both ordinary and unexpected, a mystery not to be given too much thought.

"They come, they go," she said.

Much later Megan, the animal control officer, would tell us that Mr. G. welcomed road kill, when fresh.

"If it's warm, he'll take it," she said. Once she brought him a dead deer, but had to go back to get the head for rabies testing. He came out of the house carrying the deer head by an ear. That was too much even for Megan, who asked him to put it in a bag.

To the south, Phoebe puttered about her yard, conducting an extensive reclamation project in which she was trying to eradicate her lawn. She took every packing box we had, put a layer of cardboard over the grass, then covered it with mulch from a huge mountain she kept by the big red barn behind her house. She planted perennials, forgot what they were, and pulled them up for weeds. She was a soft-spoken and cheerful conversationalist. "I am humbled," she would say about the chickens or the workmen or the plans I had for the house. "I am moved."

To the north, the Bindles, Randall and Alice, ran a rambunctious garden and had two gentle, quiet huskies. The white husky, Nutka, had blue eyes. Sheba had mismatched eyes, one brown, one blue. At night, Randall, a professional tenor, sang to them, and they howled back at him to earn their night's walk. The only thing they loved better than their walk was to escape from their fenced yard and run away. One day, Nutka, the white husky, had pushed herself against the vine-covered chain-link fence as she was trying to dig her way out. She froze there, the side of her face mashed against the fence, as we drove by. *Pay no attention*, she as good as commanded. *I am not here.*

The Bindles had parents, he a mother and she a father, who were married to each other. They had eloped in their seventies when their two grown children were dating. They were lovely people and spent part of the year with the younger Bindles.

"Nice bench," I called to Alice's father, Alfred, an industrious fellow who was a bit hard of hearing.

"He's home," he called back.

"Trying out your handiwork?" I tried again.

"Isn't it though," he said.

In the beginning we had no dryer. I went to the Laundromat for six weeks instead. I came to enjoy it a little. I could do four loads at once, throw them into two huge dryers, and an hour later the whole thing would be done except for the folding, at which I am casual, at best. I liked the assortment of people at the Laundromat, and I liked to imagine who they were and what they were doing there, and why they didn't have a washer or dryer. Upscale to downscale, on foot and in BMWs, all kinds showed up. The Laundromat was open from five A.M. to midnight every day, including holidays. I liked living in a town that could support such an establishment.

For we had moved from a town with no crime to a town in which the police log in the weekly local paper was a hotbed of information. On big weeks—Six Mile had recently seen a large cocaine bust and a small wave of heroin-related deaths—the log ran three pages, but even on a normal week it ran two. In the summer, with the influx of beachgoers and vacationers and summer residents, the log swelled to four or five pages and a uniformed police officer walked a beat between the pond and the beach.

A wide variety of items made it into the log. Many of them were amusing.

> *Caller reports an eight-year-old is mooning traffic from the window of a residence.*

> *Caller reports a man who looks very strange is in her driveway looking at tools. Officers report the man was a rake with a shirt on it and caller will be going to bed for the evening.*

School bus driver reports there is a dead possum in the street and someone has put sunglasses on it and a straw in its mouth.

A white husky from Porrazzo Road made regular appearances, usually generating several calls per week and eventually assuming mythical proportions.

Caller reports the white husky from Porrazzo Road is biting little dogs.

Multiple callers report the white husky from Porrazzo Road has been on the beach for three hours, chasing children and stealing food.

Caller reports the white husky from Porrazzo Road is loose again. This is a recurring problem. Attention ACO!

Here, in the corner of the pond and the island, we lived in a small pocket of calm. Now and then boys walked by trying to hide six-packs of beer as they rounded the corner and cut up behind Phoebe's barn to the big rock beyond. But in the town at large, more serious offenses were common. Recently, an unarmed robbery had allegedly been committed by a man who once painted my bathroom in Hearts-Are-Cold. He strolled into a local bank wearing a baseball cap as a disguise, stole an undisclosed amount of money, and made his getaway by walking down Main Street. He was quickly apprehended. But assault and battery, domestic abuse, armed and unarmed robbery, possession of dangerous weapons and class A substances, disorderly conduct, wanton destruction of property, and drunk and disorderly behavior were common fare in Six Mile. Here, everyone was not blond and I wasn't sure anyone owned a golden retriever.

A quick survey of the police logs of Hearts-Are-Cold showed that three-quarters of the entries concerned traffic violations. Other than that, youths gathered and were dispersed. Someone saw a fisher cat. The librarian retired. Their newspapers were boring, though I once saw advertised, and applied for, a job as secretary to a private investigator. I believe I was overqualified.

In the beginning, I hobbled around and things got done. I did not have time to regret, mourn, or wallow. I got up in the morning and threw open the windows and doors. I unpacked. It was the dog who had the hardest time. A few days after we moved, I went outside just in time to see her hind end rounding the corner of the street, by Mr. and Mrs. G.'s hedge, presumably hightailing it back to Hearts-Are-Cold and the only home she had ever known.

I have been lucky in my life with dogs. I was lucky at eighteen when I was given a young hound who had been plucked off the streets of New York City, and who became my companion for ten years until she disappeared, shot, I think, for chasing sheep. There were other dogs after that, but it is hard to have had the dog of a lifetime early in life. It is hard to find one who can compete with the memory of being young and free with a dog who would follow you anywhere.

In later years I was happy being a one- or two-cat household, dogless, but after the separation and before we moved to Six Mile Beach, after the gerbils died and the snake went to live at the Wildlife Center, my daughter mourned the idea of a dog. She was heartbroken.

"I want a puppy," she wailed every night.

"This is about more than a puppy," I suggested.

"I know, Mom," she cried, "but I want one." It being my first year of sorrow and guilt, I began what would become a fierce and frenzied search for a puppy, but it appeared that there were none in all of eastern Massachusetts. Then I found a shelter in the western part of the state that imported puppies from Virginia and Puerto Rico, and I called. I was told that the puppies just *flew* out of there and that people showed up two hours before opening to wait in line for them. Through a gross miscalculation of travel time, we arrived at the shelter three hours early. It was pouring. Then it was hailing. Then it was snowing. It was *May*. But we were definitely the first in line. The second in line arrived two hours and fifty minutes later, ten minutes before the shelter opened.

And then we were inside. In the first cage was a sturdy sausagelike dog that looked like a stocky, full-grown dachshund, except that she was only three months old. She had the sweetest, most worried little face on earth. I opened the door of the kennel and picked her up. She wagged her tail, licked my face twice, put her head on my shoulder, and molded her sturdy body to my chest. I never put her down.

I had known beforehand that it was a possibility, if not a probability, that my daughter would not want the same dog that I wanted. But that day my daughter never found the puppy who made her smile, who made her nod her head yes. And so, in a gesture of generosity and graciousness that still breaks my heart, even though she did not want the puppy that was now Velcro-ed to my body, she reached out and touched it and said, "Okay, Mom. We'll take this one."

I have been lucky in my life with dogs. I was lucky this late in life to have found another one I loved so much. And now my dog, who looked like a dachshund on stilts, and still had the sweetest, most worried little face on earth, was not able to trust her sense of home.

The chickens, they stayed in that coop for seven days. I was told that the confinement would make them think of the coop as home and make them want to return to it at night. I was glad for the respite. I didn't have to worry about them much in that week, when I had so much else to worry about. But by the seventh day I knew I would have to let them out. I had meant to ask my handyman, who was working on the basement, to cut a chicken door for me, but I hadn't, and now he was gone. The chickens had to come out, and I would have to do it.

I used my T square and a level to pencil in the shape of a door. I used the drill and a large bit to drill holes in each corner. My keyhole saw bit the dust immediately. Don't be fooled: It won't cut through one-inch pine. So I took the plunge into the frightening world of power saws—which I considered a sure route to dismemberment—and bought a jigsaw. I cut along the lines. I was terrified. If I did it wrong I was going to have a hole but no door and possibly fewer fingers. "That'll make quick work of it," the guy at the hardware store had said about the saw, and it did.

I attached the handle and hinges to the door. I placed the door back into the opening, matched up the other side of the hinges to the shed and screwed them in. I pulled on the handle to open the door and it wouldn't budge. I checked to see if I had somehow screwed it shut. I hadn't. It turns out that to have a door that opens and closes you need something called clearance, and I didn't have it. Clearance is that little bit of extra room that allows the thickness of the door to clear the opening, and without it you could have a door, but it wouldn't move. I needed to shave wood off the sides of the door, but first I had to get the door out of the frame. In desperation, I entered the coop, faced the little door, and kicked it hard three times. It fell out.

A plane is a beautiful tool. It is simple and effective. It is heavy and fits the hand well. Run it along the side of a pine chicken door and it slices off neat curls of wood. Do this carefully and eventually your chicken door will open. It did open. It shut. I built a cute ramp, propped it up on the sill, and opened the door. The chickens gathered in the doorway and peered into the yard for about five minutes, craning their necks. Two of them teetered on the lip of the door before jumping out, walking down the ramp, and plucking nonchalantly at the grass. The rest followed immediately. Ten minutes later the lot of them were taking dirt baths. I took pictures.

As for my daughter, she hit the ground running. She explored the neighborhood on foot and in-line skates. She went to the beach with her friends. I kept expecting her to wail suddenly in the middle of the night that she wanted to go home, but she never did. Miraculously, she was as much in awe of our shabby new house and strange little neighborhood as I was. And one afternoon after she and her friend F. had gone to the beach and then walked up to the Frosty Claw for greasy fries and really bad hot dogs, we all sat on the deck. Beach towels hung over the railings. In the distance, we could see wild flashes of lightning.

"Oh, look," said F., pointing upward.

Thousands of dragonflies flew in the air above us, above the backyard, and for hundreds of feet to the east. They did what dragonflies do, darted and spun, hovered, changed directions instantly in midair, swooped, darted, and disappeared. Thousands of dragonflies—thousands—flying over my yard.

"Dragonfly Farm," I said.

My daughter nodded. She smiled.

There were days when I couldn't believe what we had done, and days when I couldn't believe what still remained to be done. I still had my vision. It still did not match the reality. There were times when I wondered what the parents of my daughter's friends thought, driving into our driveway and comparing our tiny ragged house to their huge perfect ones. "The new windows will be here in two weeks!" I wanted to call out. Just so they'd know.

I still didn't have a desk, but we had the full moon rising behind the trees. We had Mars in its once-in-a-thousand-lifetimes visibility from Earth. And one night I saw a large ball of fire fall slowly through the air toward the pond. Maybe it was Saint Elmo's fire, or a meteor that made it through the atmosphere, and fell, still burning, into the algae-filled waters of the pond. Or maybe it was a hallucination, a distinct possibility in those mad days. I thought of calling the police to see if anyone else had seen it, but I did not. I imagined reading about it in the police log.

Youths shooting seagulls with paint-ball guns.

Man calls to say he saw a coyote. Says he will call every time he sees one.

Caller says she saw a ball of fire fall into the pond. Officer Casagrande detailed.

To the Board of Health:

I would like to apply for a permit to keep six chickens, all hens.

The hens are housed in a six-by-eight-foot "shed," which gives them eight square feet per bird. The building is new, in good condition, attractive, and clean. It has windows, shutters, and window boxes. As I have just moved in, the shed is still unpainted, but it will be painted to match my house, which is light gray with white trim. The hens also have a six-by-twelve-foot fenced yard, which they have access to during the day. At night they are securely confined to the shed.

I am enclosing a drawing, which shows the location of the shed, and yard on my property and approximate distances, based on measurements taken by a fencing company in July.

Water supply needs are met with a garden hose. Food is stored in my basement in sealed plastic storage containers. I am very careful about cleanliness. The Board of Health nurse has already viewed the chickens and their enclosures and can attest to their condition and the quality of their dwelling. The Department of Food and Agriculture Bureau of Animal Health representative has also examined the chickens and their surroundings and has approved of their condition and accommodations. I am enclosing the inspection report.

The chickens are kept as pets. This is a small group of

chickens and I will not be adding to their number. The chickens do not make noise, they do not smell, they are not a health hazard, and, when I implement my plans for the area, they will not be easily visible to neighboring properties. My plans for the area include painting the shed, planting the window boxes, putting up a white trellised fence around the chain-link fence, and planting shrubs and climbing vines.

I have spoken to the neighbors who own and live in the properties to either side, and across the street, as well as with the tenant to the back of my house, and they have no objections to the chickens.

Sincerely,
Catherine Goldhammer

Enclosed:

Drawing of property
Photograph of property
Copy of Animal Health Inspection Report
Copies of letters from abutters
Photograph of chicken house and run
Photograph of chickens

Chickens on Trial

A week later, I was on what may have been the week's fifth trip to the hardware store when my cell phone rang. It was my daughter and she was frantic.

"Someone from the Board of Health just came to the door and said there was a complaint about the chickens. She said we need a permit to keep them and that we are going to have to go to court." Since I had talked with my few neighbors about the chickens before moving in, and since there *was* no one else back there, I was confused. I told her that everything was going to be fine, although I had no such confidence. The next day I pulled into my driveway and Phoebe ran out of her front door waving.

"The animal control officer was here," she said, "and she gave me this." She handed me a yellow slip of paper. "She said they were fine," she said, "but you are going to have to go to court."

"Do you know who complained?"

"It was Mr. M.," she said, pointing toward the cottage at

the very end of the path. "He doesn't live there, but he complains a lot. Just tell me what you want me to do. Do you want me to go to court with you? Do you want me to write you a letter? Because I will." And she did.

I called Joyce, the nurse from the Board of Health who had been the one to knock on my door. She told me what I already knew, that I would have to go to a hearing. She also told me the story of Hamlet the pig, who lived on P Street, and who had, like my chickens, been the cause of a neighborly dispute. Hamlet was a very large potbellied pig and had lived on P Street for several years before a neighbor, for reasons thought to be non-pig-related, complained. Because the houses on P Street are very close together, Hamlet was nowhere *near* legal. He lived in the basement of the house, came and went through a very large dog door, and his backyard shelter was a pink plastic playhouse. Although Hamlet was initially required to move, he ultimately prevailed in the courts and was reinstated. There was once again a pig on P Street. When I relayed this story to my daughter, she brightened.

"So maybe there's hope for us," she said.

Joyce left me with the list of requirements for the keeping of poultry, and I commenced to write my request for a permit. The requirements were byzantine. One would have thought that we were planning a dairy farm. As per the land requirements, the shelter for the livestock had to be fifty feet from any house, twenty feet from all property lines, fifty feet from any public way or public water source. This made it clear that almost no one in the town of Six Mile Beach would ever be able to keep livestock legally. According to the regulations it would have been easier to have a horse in Six Mile Beach than a chicken.

I got out my hundred-foot measuring tape and we measured off our property. Our chicken coop was too close to our house and too close to Phoebe's property line. Other than that we were good. But I didn't know what we were dealing with. I didn't know the absentee landlord who had complained, or the kind of people who sat on the Board of Health, or the people of Six Mile Beach at all for that matter. Maybe they didn't like newcomers. Maybe they wouldn't like *us*. In Hearts-Are-Cold, I knew, if a well-heeled neighbor had complained about the chickens and brought us to court, I would have lost the battle when I walked in the room. Wrong clothes, wrong haircut, wrong birthplace, wrong tax bracket. I don't mean to give the impression that I was poorly dressed, ill groomed, and poverty-stricken. But Hearts-Are-Cold was very fashionable and the social strata was very high. Chickens, I am sure, were not considered desirable neighbors. But more than that, I was afraid that I had made a mistake. That I had been wrong about Six Mile Beach and the little neighborhood by the pond. That I had been betrayed by my intuition and had moved us to the wrong place after all.

Phoebe wrote me a letter stating her support for the chickens and the location of their coop. Randall Bindle wrote me a letter as well. Mr. G. told me over and over, "Just tell them they are pets," he said. "They don't care."

There is a certain kind of man who has his mind made up before he hears the question and Mr. M. was one of them. One day, shortly after his complaint, he showed up to fuss around his yard. Staking a claim, I thought. I thought that if I talked with him, it might help. And so I waved and walked over to his yard and introduced myself.

"You're supposed to have a permit," he said abruptly.

"Yes," I said. "I'm in the process of getting one."

"You were supposed to have one. You can see that I put a lot of effort into keeping my property up," he sneered. "Having a chicken coop here will make it harder to rent."

But Mr. M.'s property was all about location and nothing about upkeep. The paint was peeling, shutters were askew, and windows were warping out of their frames. I explained that if it was the asthetics of the chicken enclosure that he was worried about, I planned to put up a privacy fence and shrubs, and that once I did, he wouldn't ever even see the chickens. I didn't say that his current tenant, James, thought that the chickens were cute.

"If you do that," he said, "I'll either approve or not. I'll do whatever I am going to do."

With that remark, the gauntlet was thrown. I was done with being nice. When Mr. M. left, I got my camera, snuck onto his property, and took close-ups of his house and its disreputable windows. I added nasty paragraphs to my permit letter. I reported in to Joyce.

"I wonder if he has a permit to have a tenant in that house. Let me look," she said. "Hmmm. No, he doesn't. Not since 1997. And the last time we were in that house there were violations. I would think he'd be worried about drawing attention to himself." I heard the thunk of a large book closing.

"I talked with Kevin," she said. Kevin was the director of the Board of Health. "He doesn't think there will be a problem." A glimmer of hope had appeared.

The following day Mr. M. appeared at his property in a pickup truck and proceeded to load it up with weeds. His seven-year-old daughter, dressed all in pink, rode around the driveway on her pink bicycle. She couldn't tear her eyes away from the chickens. I could tell she was dying to see them, and I felt bad for her because I knew that for all she might beg him to let her, he never would.

I amassed my forces. Formal request for a permit, letters from neighbors, inspection report from Animal Control. Letter from public health nurse, promise from handyman to build the privacy fence once the chickens were legal. Pictures of the chickens, drawings of the yard, measurements. And finally, as an ace up my sleeve, to be used only if direly needed, the pictures of Mr. M.'s house.

The chickens went about their business, oblivious. When the dog stuck her nose through the chain link, Blackie pecked it hard and the dog jumped back and fell on the ground. They were not yet laying eggs, but it was on my mind that they soon would be. They knew nothing about Mr. M., and cared less. They were living in the moment, chasing each other after worms. And I, after all the months of selling and packing, and renovating, and moving, was tired. I hurt. My leg was still swollen and I had no feeling in parts of my shin. And although we loved Dragonfly, for all of the reasons I had thought we would, it was not yet home. I thought I would miss nothing about the house in Hearts-Are-Cold, but I did. I missed the small high windows of my bedroom. The crunch of cars driving up the pea stone driveway. The hush of the wind in the oak and maple trees that covered our yard. Dragonfly was quiet and beautiful, and at night I sometimes woke up and looked out at the chicken coop under the trees, or across the salt pond to the cottages twinkling on the other side. But I hadn't yet been able to put up pictures. Having struck out alone with my child, cat, dog, and six chickens, I was still waiting to come home. Of all of us, the chickens cared the least. They were easy to please, chickens, and they liked their new shed. But now their fate was in the hands of three people we didn't know, and after all the work along the way, now that we finally had them in what was meant to be their permanent shelter, it was possible that we wouldn't be able to keep them.

. . .

Two days before the scheduled hearing, Kevin called to arrange a home visit. I was nervous. I was a cultural trauma survivor, and I was not counting on anything. But it turned out that Kevin had a weathered face, clear blue eyes, wore a flannel shirt, and drove a pickup truck that had seen some use. Most of the pickup trucks in Hearts-Are-Cold were brand-new, big, shiny Christmas presents of trucks, and flannel was not popular. We walked over to the coop.

"That isn't fifty feet from your house," he said. "But it's your house, so that shouldn't matter. You could get a variance for that."

He took out his measuring tape.

"It's too close to her property line," I said, "but she has given me permission for that."

"Where's the property line?"

"She's not sure. Somewhere over there."

He measured. "Let's say fifteen feet. Supposed to be twenty. But she doesn't mind, so that shouldn't be a problem."

"I hope you have a lock on that," he said, pointing to the chicken run. I moved to show him how the latch to the run worked. "Or Mr. G. will be over here stealing your chickens," he said, and laughed.

"He's been so nice," I said.

"He's a sweet man," he said.

He eyed the coop and run. "Perfect place for it," he said. "Don't lose sleep over this. Say your piece but don't talk too much. They're nice people."

He took my paperwork and left, stopping first to talk with Mr. G. in the street. I could hear them from my kitchen, talking and laughing, and I felt good, but it was not over.

On August 28, one month to the day after we moved in, the Board of Health met to decide the fate of our chickens. Town Hall was comfortably small. The police department and fire station were on the lower back level, and the town offices occupied two corridors on the first and second floors. The doors at the ends of the hall were propped open with bricks. There was one small meeting room on the first floor, which was where the hearing would be held. Several worn and comfortable red leather chairs sat in the hall outside of it. My daughter and I sat down. She grabbed my hand. We wondered when the meeting would start, who would be there, and whether Mr. M. would come. We hoped not, but I expected that he would. About ten minutes before six, a man in his sixties or seventies walked down the hall and introduced himself and shook our hands. He was Mr. B., and he was on the Board of Health. He sat down next to me.

"I was out there to see them today," he said. "I thought it looked nice. I don't have any problem with it." He went inside.

Then through the door at the end of the hall came Mr. M. He walked down to our station and introduced himself, as if we had never met. I introduced him to my daughter. He commenced to restate his case to us, beginning with, "I have no desire to hurt you." And I could see that he didn't. Although what he was trying to do *would* hurt us, I could see that it wasn't his motive. His concern for his property value outweighed whatever emotional outcome his actions would have on us. He tried to be conversational and I could see that he felt awkward. My daughter's grip on my hand was beginning to hurt. Then Kevin appeared in the doorway and invited us in.

It was a small room, but official-looking. At one end there were three rows of padded chairs facing the open end of a U-shaped wooden table, at which sat the members of the Board of Health: Kevin on the left, Mr. B. in the middle, and Mrs. N. on the right. Having lived in Hearts-Are-Cold, where the median family income is in the mid–six figures, I was unprepared for the kindness of these people, for their unassuming appearance and their gentle faces. In Hearts-Are-Cold, we would not have had a chance. In this town, I could see that we did.

Kevin formally introduced the issue. I stated my case, briefly, as he had told me to. I explained the ways in which the chickens did not meet the code and the reasons why I wanted a variance for those. Then it was Mr. M.'s turn. He said that the chickens would lower the value of his property if and when he decided to sell it. He said that he put a lot of effort into keeping the property in good repair. He said that he had been shocked to see the coop when he drove by one day.

Mr. M. was wearing a maroon polo shirt with a Harvard Business School logo. They say that when a jury is about to send a guy to prison for life, they don't look at him. The members of the board didn't seem to want to look at Mr. M.

"I drove by the chickens today," said Mr. B.

"You did?" asked Kevin.

"I was out, so I thought I'd take a look," said Mr. B. "I thought they looked nice." He fiddled with some papers. "I have two young grandsons and I thought they would like to see those chickens."

"But what if I sell my property and get less for it?" said Mr. M.

"I think the chickens add to the value of the neighborhood," said Mr. B. Mrs. N. nodded almost imperceptibly.

"The house right next door to the pig's house just sold," she said. "And they got a lot. It was a very nice house."

"But a lot is a relative term," said Mr. M. "What if they got fifty thousand less than they would have if there was no pig there?"

Mrs. N. looked down and shook her head ever so slightly.

"What if we said she could only have the chickens for ten years?" said Mr. M. They all looked down.

"What if I see chickens walking all over the yard?" he said.

"The coyotes would take care of that," said Mrs. N.

"What if I hear a rooster?" he said.

"She doesn't have a rooster," said Mrs. N.

"Does this mean that there could be chickens there forever?" said Mr. M.

"She could have them there for as long as she lives," said Kevin.

"What about the abandoned truck across the street from her house?"

"Police Department," said Kevin.

"What about the abandoned boat?"

"Building Department," said Kevin.

And then, almost as an aside, barely audibly, Mr. B. said, "So do we call a motion?"

"Motion for a permit for chickens, with a variance for sections seven and eight," said Kevin.

"Which sections?" said Mr. B.

"Seven and eight."

Mr. B. looked at Mrs. N. "Fine with me," he said. She nodded. And it was over.

My daughter hugged me. Mr. M. was gracious in defeat. He said congratulations. He shook my hand, and shook my daughter's hand. He was a gentleman and a good loser after all. We left, chickens victorious, went to the Laundromat to put the laundry in the dryer, and then to the Frosty Claw for fried clams and ice cream. Dragonfly Farm would remain a farm after all. Phoebe asked me not to put up a fence because she liked to watch the chickens from her kitchen.

"It's like having fish," she said. And I, thinking of Mr. G., bought a padlock for the coop.

There were many things that could happen to these chickens. Something could dig under the fence or chew its way into the coop. We could put them in at night and forget to close the window and a raccoon could break in. They could get sick or egg-bound or die of an impacted crop. "You could put them in a padded cell," wrote one Backyard Chickens member, "and they'd still find a way to croak." There were no guarantees that these chickens would live a long life and die of natural causes in their sleep one night. But whatever their fate would be, it would befall them here, with us, on Dragonfly Farm.

Five days after the victory, I went to work at a real job for the first time in twenty years. I had been whirling for six months. I needed to stop whirling for a while, and most of me thought the way to do this was to start a new job. All the rest of me could think of was that I had nothing to wear. I used to say that I was good enough at teaching reading that I could wear a dress made out of a grain sack and it wouldn't matter. Now I would work in a tony school in an affluent town a half hour south and clothes *would* matter. I am a Henry David Thoreau kind of person, at least in the sense of "Beware any occasion that requires the buying of new clothes," and I was indeed wary. If my life was out on DVD, the women of America would be sitting in front of their television sets saying, "What is it with her and affluent towns? Don't you think she would have learned this lesson by now? Stop! Go home! Do not open that door!" Me? I went to the mall.

I admired fashionable women and I had a theoretical interest in being one. I had a stylish self-*image*, which was extravagantly at odds with my actual *self*, because I was not very interested in clothes. Not very interested in hair, really, either. I loved beauty, was obsessed about it, even. But of myself I could see only my shoes and my bag most of the time. This may be why I had a very stylish shoe and handbag life, both theoretically and actually. I would have to put some attention now into clothing. The clothes were the only thing I was worried about. The job, I knew, would be fine. I liked what I did. I liked the school system. The money, the hours, everything about it seemed ideal. The colleague who had hired me would be happy to have me there. I was about to find out how desperate he was, and why.

On my first day, a professional development day, I was given some details about my job that should have sent me packing; details that if I'd known them ahead of time would have meant that I wouldn't have taken the job at all. I was also told that my schedule had changed, and although the number of hours remained the same, they would now consume the middle of my day. I knew right away that this was not a good thing, that a half-time job that takes place in the middle of the day is about the same as a full-time job in terms of the time left. But I needed the money, and so I put my daughter into a car pool driven by a woman who wore leopard-skin pants and snakeskin boots and drove either a very old red Corvette or a very old Jeep. I would get reports on the cars from my daughter.

"The warning bells and lights are going off a lot," she said about the Jeep. The Corvette was equally dismaying, though in a different way.

"She opens it up right at the beach," she said. It took me a minute to realize what she meant.

Child, house, dog, chickens, everything else fit in around the paltry edges of my job. I got up in the morning, put my daughter into one of the two cars, got ready for work, worked, picked up my daughter, came home, and did everything else. And worse, I did not like the students or the administration. Because of the nature of my work, I spent my days in a small room, with student after student, and I was not tied into the fabric of the school. And whether it was the affluent town or the administration of the school, there was a degree of rudeness and xenophobia that surprised me.

It was the Hearts-Are-Cold feeling, the marriage feeling. Found-Wanting, it could have been called, or No-Chance-in-Hell. I was like the Jeep. All my warning bells and lights were going off. All of my little internal voices were telling me to leave. But I needed the money. So I stayed.

Ova

Meanwhile, Brownie, who looked like a hawk with a beard, was behaving strangely. Whenever we went near her, she squatted, hunched her shoulders, and froze. She was our second most skittish hen, but now we could touch her and she wouldn't move. Then, one day I let the chickens into the coop at dusk, as was my custom, and there, as I bent to close and latch the chicken door, framed perfectly in the center of the opening was a small jade-green egg sitting on the pine chips like a prize in a magical box. I knew it was Brownie's because she was the only one of my hens who would lay colored eggs. We cracked it into a small white bowl, where the bright orange yolk floated in a clear albumen sea. We scrambled and ate it, one bite apiece. Given the amount of money I had poured into those chickens and their well-being, it was a very expensive breakfast.

I felt guilty eating it, the hard labor of this small, terrified chicken who redeemed herself (I had a bit of a grudge against the ones who didn't like me) by producing this amazing pale green egg. I saved the broken shell. I soaked it in soap and water and put it on a bed of paper towel inside a pretty jar that in another lifetime had held a very expensive olive tapenade. Later we learned that our hen squatted because she saw us, in effect, as roosters. I was disappointed about this, having thought that she just liked us all of a sudden, that she had magically become tame. We also learned that this meant she was sexually mature and would start laying soon, which by then we already knew. All over America, spring chickens were laying eggs.

Hens lay all kinds of eggs. Some first eggs are tiny, the size of a grape. Some have small yolks, double yolks, or no yolks at all. An egg can have a fragile shell, a rocklike shell, or a shell enclosed in another shell, but I am told this is extremely rare. There are eggs with chalky shells, glassy shells, oddly shaped or wrinkled shells, soft shells, and no shells at all. Some hens eat their own eggs right up, shells and all. Some say that if you blow an egg and fill it with hot mustard, it will break them of the habit. Others just eat the offender, problem solved.

Each egg is different. Eventually we got blue eggs and green eggs, pink eggs and brown eggs. We got whitish eggs, speckled eggs, freckled eggs, and eggs with white patches. We had one enormous egg with two yolks, and a wide variety of other sizes: small and oval, big and round, tall and thin. Sometimes I found eggs that had just been laid, warm and slightly damp. Finding a warm egg felt miraculous. Putting a warm egg into someone's unsuspecting hand was like handing them the moon.

I can guarantee you that the eggs you pull out of the nesting box are better, prettier, and more delicious than anything you will ever buy in a store, free-range or not. The eggs you buy in the supermarket can be as much as three months old. An egg whose white spreads out thinly into the pan is an old egg. A hard-boiled egg that is hard to peel is a new egg. An egg that sinks in a bowl of water is fresh; an egg that floats, don't eat.

But was my use of their eggs sentencing them to perpetual laying, trying to make up what I had taken? Was collecting their eggs throwing them into panic? Was I stealing their imaginary babies? I pored through my chicken books and discovered that I was not.

A hen is born with two ovaries and four thousand undeveloped eggs. In time the right ovary will atrophy and the left ovary will lie along her backbone to a point midway between her neck and her tail. She will begin to lay at around twenty weeks, one egg every three days or so at first, smaller eggs to start. She will eventually lay, on average, six eggs a week. She will lay on a twenty-five-hour cycle. An hour after an egg is laid, a new egg ovulates, and the shell of the next egg to be laid is calcified. If she lays at nine in the morning on Tuesday, she will likely lay at ten on Wednesday. She will continue to cycle through the day until, since she won't like to lay in the dark, she will wait to begin the cycle anew the next morning.

I remember once, I must have been a child, on my grandparent's farm, my grandmother dressing out a chicken.

"Look," she said. And there within the chicken was a line of golden yolks, each increasing in size, until at the end a shelled egg lay in wait. I remember being shocked because, there inside of a chicken was one of the most beautiful things I had ever seen, a line of golden suns.

People are often surprised to learn that hens lay eggs without the assistance of a rooster. Of course, like all females, they have the eggs, but they need the rooster to get the babies. Many people think that the small spot of white on the side of an egg yolk indicates that it is fertilized, but, in fact, all eggs have that spot. It is called the blastoderm and it is the location on the egg yolk where the sperm would attach if a sperm were present. If this spot is irregularly shaped, the egg is not fertile. If it is round with a small dark speck, it is an embryonic chicken and the dark speck is its eye.

Having the rooster guarantees that the eggs you collect will, most likely, be fertile, but it does not guarantee that your hens will sit on them. The desire of hens to sit on eggs is determined not by the act of producing eggs, but by hormones. If a hen is hormonally inclined, she will "set." If not, she won't. A hen who wants to set is called "broody" and she will set on anything. She will set on her own eggs or on someone else's. They don't have to be fertile and they don't have to be chicken eggs. She will set on fake eggs, no eggs, apples, rocks, or golf balls. Once a hen wants to set, she will stay in a nest, fluff up her feathers, and she will not want to leave. She will get mad if you try to get her out of there. She will stop laying eggs, whether or not there are any underneath her. In her mind, she is done laying until the current batch, imaginary or not, are hatched out. A broody hen can be "broken up," or jolted out of her desire to set, by taking away whatever she is sitting on, by taking her away from the nest, or taking the nest away from her. But if allowed to set on fertile eggs, she will take care of whatever hatches, whether chickens or ducks, geese or guinea hens. If she is sitting on an empty nest or infertile eggs, she can be given newly hatched chicks and she will take care of them.

So our chickens were doing what they were meant to do, laying their eggs, and we were doing our part in eating them. They appeared to be somewhat proud of them, and Blackie and Big Yellow seemed to like sitting on their eggs for a few minutes, but our chickens didn't think they were their babies. If we didn't take their eggs, they would keep on laying until the nest was full, and then they would lay on the floor. Someone I know has a bowlful of teensy little eggs laid by their zebra finch. Same deal.

And as for roosters, I don't really know much. I have heard they are comical. They are territorial. A good rooster will protect his hens from predators. I have heard of one rooster who kept a possum cornered all night and once killed a hawk. A bad rooster considers its owner a competitor or a predator and can inflict serious damage. They crow, and some crow all night. I was not allowed to have roosters and I had no desire to push for one. I would have virgin hens blithely laying perfect eggs about which they cared only a little.

The Window

I put the kitchen in backward. The windows should have come first, then the plastering. Then the floor, the hookups for the appliances, and finally the cabinets. But I didn't figure that out until the new cabinets were already in. This was akin to filling a living room with new furniture when you still had to rip out the walls. The cabinets looked wonderful, pristine and white, but the far wall of the kitchen was still covered with brown glue. The wall over the lower cabinets on the window side was pockmarked with holes and uneven layers of wallboard. A corroded pipe stuck through a two-foot hole in the ceiling. A dirty sock was stuffed into the pipe. The floor was still the old floor: stained, peeling, chipped linoleum with a nine-foot U-shaped scar in it.

"It's okay," said my friend Christopher, the cabinetmaker who had built our kitchen table, which stood forlorn and tarp-shrouded in the middle of the chaos. "It's just a kitchen." His wife had just had a baby, so things like kitchens were secondary in the first blush of new parenthood.

"It'll get done," he said. "You're just a couple of workmen away from being finished." He got an enormous level from his truck and laid it every which way on the cabinets.

"Everything's level," he said. "That's good."

I had done many things to this house, but the kitchen was the biggest change I would make, and I was afraid. We had gotten used to not having a stove, to eating takeout and salads, and bad stir-fries cooked up on the hotplate. We had gotten used to stepping over the hole in the floor. Now we were without a sink as well. We were without usable cupboards. And I was about to cut a huge hole into the back wall of our house for a nine-foot window and a wide-open look at the pond.

From the beginning, from the moment I decided to buy the house, I had envisioned a huge set of windows over the sink counter, but no one seemed to share my vision. It may have been the cost involved or the anticipated headache of doing it, but everyone tried to talk me out of that window.

"Why don't you put two little half windows to either side of the one you already have," said Sage.

"Just put in one window to the right of the sink and leave the one you have," said Penny.

"That window looks just fine to me," said Scarlet.

I knew that the window would cost me. First, it was going to be expensive. Second, I would have to cut into the shell of the house for the first time, and I wasn't sure that would be a good thing. I had no idea what was under the vinyl siding. I feared asbestos shingles or severe rot or peeling lead paint, and most of me didn't want to know. But I had bought not just a house, but a house with an imaginary nine-foot window over the sink, so I ordered it, along with replacements for every other window in the house.

When the windows came, two nice young men named Chris and Scott spent two days installing the replacements. Chris, the lead, was dark and well-spoken. Scott looked like he'd just walked out of college. They had a system and it was clean and fast. On the afternoon of the second day, they faced the kitchen counter and tore the wallboard off the interior wall.

"They should have checked for wires here," said Scott.

They *should* have checked, because two huge electrical conduits ran from counter to ceiling on either side of the existing window. Big wires. I called Rick and begged him to look at it. He rearranged appointments for me. I have had good luck with my workmen, although Doug, the plumber, had taken to disappearing for periods of time. His answering machine did not answer. All along he had shown up at odd times, mostly without calling. His truck would pull into the parking space across the street among the overgrown grape vines, next to the monster truck, and he would appear at my door, deferential and polite, and do the next thing to be done. He had been a godsend, and I adored him. Now I needed him to put in the connections for the appliances. I needed him to knock the top of the big pipe out of the ceiling. I needed him badly, and at the moment he was nowhere to be found.

But Rick and Rich showed up first thing in the morning in their red trucks. They examined the wires. I listened from the rocking chair in my bedroom, fearful of the outcome. They spoke electrician.

"This one's hot," said Rick.

"This one's neutral," said Rich.

"This must be red and this one must be white."

"These are both white."

"I've got seven volts over here."

"That's impossible."

"Did I say this one was neutral?"

"Does that one go upstairs or up over the ceiling and down to that one over there?"

"This doesn't make any sense."

"I've got no power over here for these lights. What happened to that?"

They proceeded to pull wires out of the walls. They moved the refrigerator and did something behind it. They conferred with the window guys. Either it couldn't be done, in which case they would take back the window, which was

ghastly expensive, and put in one that would fit the space between the wires, or it could be done, and I would be living
with chaos either way, a wall stripped down to the wood, the
house filled with cold air and fog moving in off the ocean.

"It's impossible to raise the outlets," Rick told me, "but
we can move the wires." I got on the phone to Rob, the
counter guy. "Don't make the backsplash," I told him. "They
can't move the outlets."

"No problem," he said, "but I want to put it in on Friday."

"I'll see what I can do," I told him, but actually, I didn't. The
plasterer wanted to plaster before the counter was in and
there was no chance things would be ready for him before Friday. "Give me a couple of days' notice," he had said. I had
called him on Wednesday to ask him to be there on Friday, but
I had no idea if he could be. I still hadn't ordered the floor. Until the floor went in, I had no appliances. I had no *sink*.

"It's just a kitchen," Christopher had said. I knew that, although I thought him baby-addled, and I wanted my sink
back. I had been cooking with a hot plate and countertop
oven for three months and didn't mind a bit. But washing
dishes in a bucket in the bathtub for ten days had done me in.
Don't let them fool you: No matter how many paper plates
and cups and plastic utensils you use, you still need to wash
dishes.

• • •

In the meantime the whole wall above the new cabinets was stripped to the studs.

"Are you replacing the ceiling?" asked Rick.

I stared at him in disbelief.

"I guess not," he said. "I'll try to make only a small hole in it."

Chris and Scott were outside pulling siding off the house. I could hear Chris whistling. I found this reassuring. They didn't seem to be worried at all. Now Rick was whistling also. I returned to my bedroom. I heard drilling. I heard cursing. I heard sawing. I could no longer tell who was talking. "Beautiful," said someone, but he sounded sarcastic. The exposed wood on the inside of the house had looked good, solid, and free of rot or mold. I still didn't want to see the outside. Our life in this house was about to change. It would be like moving in again, to the house I had imagined when I bought the house it was.

Rick was pounding something through the ceiling.

"I don't know why these guys used to use this junk," he said. I hoped he didn't also say that it was rotting. I thought I might stay in my room forever, with my hands over my ears, mute and invisible. I was going to wait until they had cut the hole for the window and had seen everything there was to see. I was going to wait until the worst was over. Until there were no more problems. The plumber would come. The plasterer would come. The counter would come. The floor would go in. We would have a sink. We would have a stove.

We would be able to cook, although only one of us really liked to. Then I would come out, bank account depleted.

Fear is a poor companion. It gives no rest. It had been with me for some time, and I was weary of it, but I didn't know how to rid myself of its company. "MEDITATE," I wrote at the top of my list every day, and every day I didn't. I had a hard time sitting still in the most restful of times. Now, in these times, full of stress and worry, sitting still was nigh impossible. I made some effort every day to take a couple of deep breaths and get a sense of my head actually being attached to my body. At all other times it was a free-for-all in which the tornado of my anxious thoughts won handily over my body, with its aching leg and need for rest, and spun wildly into the unknown. I would learn, eventually, that everything did work out. It would have been nice to have known it in the process, while the pipe with the sock in it was still sticking through the ceiling.

At about three, when I had to leave to pick up my daughter from school, I walked out of my bedroom and into the kitchen to see the window guys standing there eating steaming subs, looking at the pond through a ten-by-four-foot hole. My dog sat on the floor next to them watching them eat.

Two days later there was a lunar eclipse. In Six Mile Beach the moon rises in the east, out of the ocean, casting a pathway of light over the water. It rises behind the single row of cottages across the pond, dwarfing them, huge and orange. And then it rises over the pond. It rises forever, it seems, for hours, over what would eventually be my orchard, what would eventually be my garden, my raspberry patch, the peonies surrounding the imaginary dipping pool. At six, on the day of the eclipse, Alesh, the young Czech painter, showed up in the dark and rain to look at the new windows and think about painting them. He had a wide Slavic face and light blond hair. He was about twenty.

"He's cute," I said to my daughter after he left.

"Mom, he's ancient," she said to me. To her friend M., on the phone, she said, "My mother has a crush on the painter." A few hours later, when the sky had cleared, we sat on the scarred floor of the unfinished kitchen and watched the moon rise and cover with shadow.

Transformations

The inside of the house was finished. Everything I had planned to do, I had done. The bathroom and the floors, the windows and the wood stove, and screen doors that slapped shut when you let them go. The kitchen was unrecognizable. At the end of the second week in November, a new hardwood floor, the color of warm honey, transformed my house. Chris came back to put the molding around the kitchen window. When I came home I found a note. "This is beautiful," it said.

My mother came for Thanksgiving, bringing with her a large turkey and all the side dishes, even though we were going out for dinner with my ex-husband and his extended, blended family. Our separation was still finding its rhythm. We were slowly finding our way to the vision of our family continuing, albeit in a different form. And so, on Thanksgiving afternoon, we met at the exclusive club where, for the duration of our marriage, we had consented to spend all of his family holidays that involved large meals. While most of the adults clustered at one end of the table, I found myself at the other with my daughter; Greg, a slightly stern Episcopalian priest; and his two children: a thirteen-year-old girl having what looked like an unhappy day, and an eighteen-year-old dark-haired boy with a quiet gaze and a deep voice. I made efforts at conversation, none of which progressed. My daughter was already saturated with my talk, and the other two were—at least on this day—not outgoing. Greg persisted in trying to draw them out, which was painful, but he did not give up, and in time a far-ranging conversation covered such topics as Britney Spears's moral compass or lack thereof, music, God, and baseball.

"There is no middle ground with God," said Greg.

"I'm an agnostic," said my daughter loudly. All heads turned to look down the table.

"He's a priest," said my ex-husband.

"That's okay with me," she answered.

The next day we cooked our turkey at home. My mother bustled about. I was afraid that the new stove would set the wall on fire. After almost eleven months of worrying, I found it hard to stop.

In early December a group of young men pulled up in an old car and swarmed all over the monster truck. One of them climbed into the cab and turned the ignition. Billows

of white, oily smoke poured out of the tailpipe and surrounded the truck in a large cloud that then blew into my
front yard. It had started, but it wasn't going to move, and
just as suddenly the young men piled into their old car and
drove away. Soon a large tow truck returned and took the
monster truck away. And then our first Christmas in our
new house was upon us.

I was frantic for things to be as they had always been. We
would have a tree and play the Vince Guaraldi Trio's record-
ing of *A Charlie Brown Christmas*. Al and Elsa, our good neighbors and fellow eccentrics from Hearts-Are-Cold, would
come for Christmas Eve and we would open presents in the
morning. We would go to our friends' house in the city for
the afternoon. The dog and the cat would have stockings.
They would receive their bones and catnip mice. We would,
as we had done the one other Christmas of our separation,
spend it together, as a family. But first, my daughter and I
would pick out a live Christmas tree. I don't know why I always expected this to be easy. I lived with a child whose visions of Christmas trees were very large.

We set out for the many fields of Tree-Berry Farm,
where we indeed found many large trees. My daughter
named each tree she liked after a character in *A Tale of Two
Cities*. Sidney Carton, Madame Defarge, Doctor and Lucie
Manette, Jarvis Lorry, Jerry Cruncher, Jacques, Jacques, and
Jacques. They were all huge, eight or nine feet tall, and if

they were not tall they were round, some of them easily seven feet across. Those trees would take up much of our new living room. (They would, for that matter, have taken up much of our *old* living room.) They would need to be folded in half to fit through the door. But in her mind's eye those trees would fit in our house, or perhaps her vision was strong enough that the logistics just didn't matter.

"Look at this one," I said, pointing out a modest little tree.

"No," she said, pointing to yet another huge tree. "Charles Darnay."

We wandered the farm for two hours, field after field, turning from one tree to another and back again, comparing, trying to return to ones we were sure we would find again, but could not. Then we saw a tree we both liked.

"The Vengeance," said my daughter.

"I don't really want a Christmas tree called The Vengeance," I said.

She looked at me. "She led the revolution, Mom."

We fetched the grizzled tree cutter, who walked over with his chain saw, and cut The Vengeance down.

"That's a big one," he said.

We took her up to the machine that shook the loose needles off.

"That's a two-person tree," said the guy, and went to find help.

I pointed out my car, the one without a roof rack.

"We can't put a tree this big on a car without a roof rack," said one of the men. "You'll never make it home."

And so, at seven that night, a large pickup truck driven by a small seventy-year-old man arrived at our house. The three of us carried The Vengeance through the front door to the living room, where the tree stand was waiting.

"I just deliver them," he said. "I don't put them up." But he helped me set it down in the tree stand before he left. We had a really big tree stand, made for a really big tree, but it was no match for The Vengeance. When I tightened the screws, the whole thing fell over. The tree was too heavy for us to pick up and recenter. I had only one option. I dragged The Vengeance out through the front door, stand and all, across the lawn, down the driveway, and up the stairs to the deck, where I stood her in a corner. The wind, precursor to a big northeaster, promptly blew her over. My daughter managed to hold her steady while I tied The Vengeance to two deck railings with four lengths of rope. The next day she still stood, albeit atilt and bowed with snow, and I went out looking for a new tree.

I didn't find one. They all looked scruffy and lopsided and bare. So I went home, got out my leather gloves and a saw, and cut four feet off the bottom of The Vengeance. I dragged her back around the house, through the front door, and set her into the stand. I surrounded her with towels. I filled pails with the ice from her branches. She looked great. My daughter came home from school, and she approved.

Up until then I had done nothing to the outside of the house. As bad as the inside had been, the yard was worse in its own barren way. There was no path to the front door. Wires snaked up the wall by the side door. There was no mailbox except for a covered basket on the side steps, dark with mold and mildew. A stack of rocks cemented into a small pillar attended the entrance to the driveway. When I bought the house and moved in, a statue of Mary in a half shell stood on the pillar.

"Do you wanna da Madonna?" asked Mrs. G., and we agreed that she would take her.

"I will put her over there," she said, pointing to her back-yard, "and she will look after you, too." She and Mr. G. came over, put Mary into a wheelbarrow, and carried her away.

Now the pillar stood bare, surrounded by the long stems of withered hosta blossoms, under a dead pine tree. I set a birdbath on it. I hammered a nail into the vinyl siding and hung a wreath. I filled a large galvanized washtub with the boughs I had cut off of the bottom of The Vengeance. I bought a mailbox, street numbers, and a doormat. The outside of the house began to look like someone cared about it. We weren't home yet, but we were closer. Christmas came, and we were all right.

After the holidays, our lives became almost normal. I was released from the weight of my job for two weeks and felt

the burden of depression lift from my shoulders. I had time
again to notice how my daughter had changed really quickly,
or so it seemed to me, from a twelve-year-old child to a
twelve-year-old woman. True to her nature, she was not going to walk that path calmly. She was not me. She loved
clothes. She loved shopping. She was lean and tall and beautiful. Anything she put on looked good on her. She was also
fearless and impulsive, prone to want red hair one week and
white-blonde hair the next, and so I had to draw certain lines
in the sand early. She could not have any piercings other than
ears while she still lived in my house. She could not have tat-
toos. She could not permanently dye her hair any unnatural
shade. But although in my opinion she was so beautiful that
makeup was unnecessary, I was not going to fight that battle.
For the most part she was eccentric but sensible, and her
taste was usually unerring. One day in the consignment shop
she went into the dressing room to try on a little black rayon
jacket with a shawl collar, a single button, and a peplum
waist. In a few minutes the door opened and there she stood
with her hands on her hips.

"Meet my new best friend," she said, and twirled. She
looked like she had just walked off a runway in Paris.

After Christmas she decided to have a party, and I was
secretly victorious. Many of her friends had large and fancy
houses on prestigious streets in wealthy towns. One beautiful and gracious house had a movie theater, an upstairs hallway bigger than my living room, and a living room bigger

than my house. But I had made something good for her, and although our street was neither prestigious nor our town wealthy, and the houses were small and some of them shabby, and our backyard was homely, the inside of our house was beautiful and welcoming and awash with light, and my daughter was no longer embarrassed to have her friends over. The night of the party the girls laughed, and the boys fought over the overstuffed rocking chairs in the living room, and some of the mothers seemed envious of the Moon Women sitting at my kitchen table, drinking tea, and wearing brightly colored scarves.

Chickens in Winter

I did not winterize the coop. I didn't insulate, run electricity, or install a heated water bowl. Completing the inside of the house was challenge enough. I didn't have another project in me, and the prevailing wisdom said that the chickens would be fine for the winter. So the coop would have to wait until next year, and that seemed all right because for an uncommonly long time, through December, it remained well above freezing. There was one northeaster and then another, a lot of snow, which promptly melted, and then quite a bit of rain. The chicken run turned into a slimy muddy sponge. The inside of the coop was equally dismaying. The pine chips became soggy and then solidified into a cementlike substance. Entering the coop threw me immediately into a depression. I wanted happy warm chickens in a clean dry coop. I wanted a sunny, grassy run with good drainage.

Then one night the temperature dropped into the low twenties. The muddy run froze solid overnight. The pine chips were frozen. The water was frozen. The food was cold.

The chickens went out for a few minutes and then hunkered down inside. The cold weather held.

In the mornings, I poured oats into a bowl and soaked them in hot tap water. I filled a plastic cup with cracked corn and a two-gallon pitcher with warm water. Then I dressed for the journey. On an average day I wore long underwear, a fleece outer layer, a down coat, a neck warmer, a hat, and fur-lined boots. An average day was in the twenties. Anything in the thirties was balmy. Really cold was single or negative numbers. Wind was the enemy.

Once dressed, I carried my offerings to the coop, where six freezing chickens in a feeding frenzy mobbed me for the oatmeal. I filled the feeder and collected eggs. There were about three eggs a day now, rather than six, and sometimes they were frozen. I took the water bowl outside, cracked the ice out of it, which took two to four good whacks, and filled it with the warm water. I promised the chickens that next year they would have a water heater and a heat lamp, an insulated coop, and a dry run. I felt bad for them. They didn't know that this would pass. They didn't know anything.

At night they huddled together in a corner and my daughter begged me to bring them into the basement. I was tempted, but even in my guilt-ridden heart, I knew that would be a mistake. I knew that once I started down that road I would be carrying those chickens inside one by one every night and carrying them out in the morning. I left them where they were, but late on the first really cold night my daughter wept. "What if they are out there, fallen over, and frozen solid? What if they are *dead*?" I trudged out to the coop with a flashlight and made sure they were still alive. They were huddled together, as usual, and when I put my hands into their midst, I felt their heat. I knew that they were wearing down coats, but I wished they were wearing wool hats and boots as well.

Then, right when it got colder than it had been in forty-seven years, my daughter left her toothbrush at her father's house. The first night, I told her to brush with her finger. The second day, it didn't occur to me until bedtime that her father had forgotten to drop off her toothbrush. She burst into tears. It was almost midnight and 0 degrees Fahrenheit, but I would drive to the super-grocery in Hearts-Are-Cold to buy a toothbrush.

"I'll be back in twenty minutes," I told her.

"You can't leave me here," she said. She was usually intrepid, but something about the hour and the temperature and the wind made it impossible. We dressed in fleece from head to toe with windproof outer layers, and drove to the store. Someone stocked groceries. Someone rode around on a floor-washing machine. Someone manned the checkout. Other than that: empty. We bought two toothbrushes—in the event of a future shortage—a box of oatmeal, and the newest issue of *Vogue*. We exchanged small talk with the checkout guy, went to our illegally parked car, and drove home. My daughter brushed her teeth for ten minutes and went to bed.

The next day, the weathermen said, would be "really cold." Having just endured eight days that ranged from 4 above to 8 below, the generality of "really cold" just sounded cruel. Zero degrees all day, with windchill down to 30 below, negative 10 at night with more wind. At midnight, when I went out with a flashlight to check the chickens, I discovered that one of the red hens had frostbite. The tips of her comb were black. I knew that the universal preventive and treatment for frostbitten combs was Vaseline. I didn't have any. Neosporin would do, but I didn't have any of that, either. For the second time in two days, we dressed at midnight. Even more fleece, more layers. We drove to the all-night super-grocery and again parked in an illegal space right next to the door. The same shelf stocker, the same machine rider, and the same guy at the checkout. He seemed like a nice enough person, but we had hoped it would be someone else. We were impossible not to recognize. We were the same mother and daughter dressed head to toe in fleece and Gortex. I told him what the Vaseline was for. He gave me my change.

Back at home, we gathered a flashlight, two battery-powered lanterns, the Vaseline, and headed for the coop. It was so cold that anything made of wood—the trees, our deck, the Bindles' fence—made loud and terrifying cracking sounds. The wind howled, and from across the pond we could hear the roaring of the ocean. Inside the coop it felt only a little warmer. I have never felt as bad for another creature as I did for those chickens that night. It was too cold, I wasn't going to bring them in, and we had to put Vaseline all over their combs.

I caught and held. My daughter greased. We became efficient. I caught a chicken, pinned it under my left arm with its feet resting on my left hand. I held my right hand on its chest, preventing escape from the front. My daughter carefully smeared Vaseline onto the combs. The smaller chickens were shivering. I tucked the frostbitten chicken under my coat for a while, and she did not object.

The next day, I drove to the feed store and bought bales of straw and made a little igloo out of them. I hauled a fifty-pound sack of layer pellets and poured it into the feed bin. I collected five eggs. I fixed the roost. For the first time in six days, they would go outside. They stormed the door when it was opened, and later, in the sunny part of the afternoon, I saw them all bathing happily in the frozen dust. My daughter and I stacked a cord of firewood and fired up the new wood stove.

"We're rural now," she said. I took a picture of her by the stacked wood, with Phoebe's red barn and the chicken coop in the background. It looked rural to me.

I began to flag at the end of January. After making it through the weeks of really cold weather, the single and negative digits, I faltered in the mid-twenties that followed. I woke up one morning and didn't want to take care of the chickens, though of course I did. The next morning, the same, and the morning after that. I was depressed about the job, I knew that. Every day I went to work and sat in the parking lot and thought, "I can't go in there." A little voice in my head said, "*Don't* go in there." It said, "This is not what you are supposed to be doing." It had been telling me that for months, but in I went.

On the third day that I burned out on the chores, I let the chickens out into the run, went into the coop to get the water bowl, and stepped back outside to knock the ice out of it. Because they were in the run guzzling oatmeal, I didn't worry that the coop door was slightly ajar. The dog, who likes projects, stood nearby watching. Suddenly, one of the red hens appeared in the doorway and, quick as you please, hopped right outside onto the doorstep. Stunned, the dog, the chicken, and I all froze. In a fraction of a second I envisioned the chicken stepping off the stoop, the dog releasing from her surprise, and generations of hound instincts kicking in. I envisioned trying to catch the chicken, not being able to, and my daughter's face when I told her.

In the following two seconds, I screamed, swooped my arms toward the chicken, slipped, and fell flat on my back. The door flew completely open behind me. Prone, and unable to see what was going on, I grabbed the door, rolled out of its way, and slammed it shut, hoping that the chicken had moved in time. I labored to my feet and looked at the run. The chicken had rejoined its companions at the oatmeal bowl, and was pretending that nothing had just happened. I filled the water bowl, clipped the coop door shut, and turned for the house.

And although the chicken did not escape, the dog had good manners, and I was not injured, I felt utterly defeated by the whole incident. I felt defeated by the cold, by the wood chips that were always stuck to my clothes and the kitchen floor, by the oatmeal, the groin muscle I suspect I had pulled hauling the bales of straw, the frostbitten combs, the midnight trips to the supermarket, the Vaseline, the weather reports, and the stiffness spreading through my body.

Leonardo, who had come to my house three times now on flood-related business, told me that his aunt had chickens.

"I tell her that it's time to get rid of them. I tell her that she doesn't need that kind of work."

I nodded.

"She says to me, 'They're what gets me out of bed in the morning.'"

I raised my eyebrows.

"She's ninety-three," he said.

I sighed. I told myself that if Leonardo's ninety-three-year-old aunt could do it, I could do it. The chickens were necessary to us. It wasn't even a possibility that we could do without them. But maybe I was doing it entirely wrong. Maybe there were changes I could make. But there, in the middle of the coldest winter in forty-seven years, which I now knew was going to last forever, thinking about changes seemed too much to bear.

Two days later, I bought an eighty-foot construction-grade extension cord, a metal construction lamp, a 250-watt heat bulb, several s-hooks, hangers, and hook-and-eye latches. I ran the cord across the yard to the coop. Armed with my drill and boxes of bits, I put on my work gloves, drilled the necessary holes, put a latch on the inside of the door, and hooked up the electricity. Then I turned on the lamp. It was so much easier to do than I thought it would be in the days before the cold hit, when the thought of picking up another tool or putting on those gloves or making another trip to the hardware store was more than I could bear.

That night I looked out of my house at the square of yellow light that was the window of the coop and felt a deep relief. I could hear the chickens celebrating. The next morning, the water was frozen around the edges, but not in the middle. It would take three days for the coop to warm up enough so that the entire bowl remained unfrozen overnight.

I should have done it sooner. It would never be that cold again for the rest of the winter. The frostbite on the combs blackened and the comb tips fell off. The door to the coop remained frozen. To close it I had to give it a good slam with my right hip. Only once did I do so with eggs in my pockets.

If You Can See the Ocean

If you stood in our kitchen, at a certain spot near the sink, and looked out the middle window, you would see that one of the cottages on the other side of the pond had a bright blue space on either side of it. That was the ocean. If one day I tore out the back wall of the second floor and installed floor-to-ceiling windows, we would have a really good view. Someone in the battle over how to manage the shorelines of America had a saying: *If you can see the ocean, the ocean can see you.* It wasn't until I weathered my first storm in Six Mile Beach that I really understood what they meant.

In the hurricane of 1938, the houses on the coast of Connecticut, where I grew up, were broken to bits and washed out to sea. Katharine Hepburn's childhood home at Fenwick went. And less famously, not famously at all actually, the summer cottage of my father's parents also went. If a hurricane of that kind were to hit the northeastern coast today, technology would provide warnings and the loss of life would be minimal. The loss of property would be huge. We have forgotten about weather. We have built houses on the beach. The sea captains of older days knew: They built their houses on hills. Along the beaches of Six Mile, especially the one closest to our house, there were cottages directly on the ocean. There were also the empty lots of the houses that used to be there, the ones washed away in the blizzard of 1978 or the No Name Storm of 1991.

It is always windy somewhere in Six Mile Beach. In Hearts-Are-Cold, our house was in a direct line of the prevailing winds, coming out of the northwest. Those winds were cold, ripping across the harbor and cove and directly across our yard. They blew away the fall leaves and made our wind chimes ring all the time. But in a storm, the winds coming out of the northeast did not affect us there. Dragon-fly Farm was a mile and a half from our old house, but in a northeaster it was in another country entirely.

The first northeaster hit early, depositing two feet of snow over much of New England. At our house we had little snow because the wind was blowing it away. By noon of the first day, my daughter could go outside, lean her whole weight against the wind, and it would hold her up. At six P.M., when, insanely, I drove her to the other end of Six Mile, it was dangerous to open the car doors. She had to hold on to something or be blown down. As we drove down the peninsula, the wind immediately decreased. By the time we got to my daughter's friend's house, the wind was strong by normal standards but nothing like what we had going on at home.

I would find out later that in our neighborhood the winds were clocked at seventy-five miles an hour. The wonderful new windows didn't rattle. They bowed. Houses across the pond were being hit by rocks. The road between the pond and the ocean was closed. Two days later, when the storm shut itself down, the big earthmovers came out to bulldoze the boulders and sand out of the road. They put it right into those empty lots where houses had once been.

On the third day after the storm, when the road was again passable, the ocean off Black Rock Beach was brown and wild. I got a call from a friend.

"Go down to the beach," he said. "There are lobsters all over it."

I had heard that after the blizzard of '78 people picked lobsters off Six Mile Beach, and I had imagined a few big lobsters here and there along the stretch of white sand. But it was nothing like that. It was dead low tide. The chocolate-colored ocean pounded the shore, but the two hundred feet of sand between the seawall and the waves was almost entirely covered with lobsters and starfish. It was near dark when I got there, and the big lobsters were gone, snagged by the early comers, the ones who knew to go looking or the ones like my friend who happened upon it by chance. "People are getting greedy," he had said. "People are carrying buckets of two-pound lobsters off the beach." Later, when I asked him, he would tell me that he himself had carried off ten and neglected to invite me for dinner.

But large swaths of sea life remained. Starfish the size of dinner plates; starfish the size of fingernails, and every size in between. Lobsters several inches long and lobsters the length of a finger. All of the starfish appeared to be dead. Many of the lobsters were also dead, but some were still alive, moving sluggishly, going nowhere. Instead of happily carting home a lobster or two, I walked among the wreckage. A few people were still looking for big lobsters. The next night, when I took my daughter to show her, ten or twenty people in small groups of two or three combed the beach with flashlights and buckets, picking through the piles of debris, collecting the smaller lobsters for gumbo or chowder or bisque. In a square yard of beach, you could find thousands.

There were other secrets about the ocean, things no one told you and that you would not see unless you were there every day, day after day, things you might not believe. There were days when cliffs and cities appeared on the horizon where no cliffs or cities had existed before. When I told my daughter about these phenomena, she told me that I must have a brain tumor. Then she saw them herself. It would be months before we found out, from someone at the Lifesaving Museum, that those were real cities, the cities of the North Shore, but that they were visible only on certain days. When I told the Moon Women about this on our next full moon, sitting at one of the dingy picnic tables at the beach, eating our salads, they didn't believe me.

"Out there?" they said, pointing to the open ocean that seemingly stretched forever, or at least all the way to France.

"That's north," I told them, and it seemed impossible for it to be north because it seemed so much like east. "That's east," I said, pointing to what should have been south, toward Black Rock Beach, and our house, and the heart of weather.

It wasn't until that first storm that I understood the geography of the coastline in Six Mile Beach. There were four official beaches and all of them were within an eighth of a mile of our house. I had always thought that Six Mile was the most vulnerable, that it was the one a storm would really hit hard. But I had been wrong. Six Mile was protected by the land across the way, the land you could only see on certain crystal-clear days, usually in winter. In the first storm I learned that it was Black Rock and Gunrock, both right across the pond from our house, that were most in harm's way.

The beach Six Mile Beach is known for, and named for, was a long, sandy crescent. At high tide there was no sand and the ocean broke over the seawall. The police log reported that baby whales and dolphins and seals washed up on Six Mile Beach that winter, but I never saw one, though I walked my dog on the seawall four days a week. The winter beach walkers had a kind of anonymous and silent community. I saw the same people and the same dogs. The old guy with the old pug, the woman with the frightened black spaniel, and the one whose bichon frise, in its dark blue fleece coat, was better dressed than I. One woman wore a knee-length skirt, colorful tights, and dapper shoes every single day. One man—I came to think of him as the mayor of the seawall—spoke to everyone who passed. "How are you?" he'd say in a deep, hearty voice. "How are you doing?"

One day in late winter, I went for my customary walk, only to find about half the boardwalk fenced off. Big signs proclaimed DANGER: SEAWALL MAY COLLAPSE. I walked around the fence to the place about halfway down, in front of the pavilion, where one could regain the sidewalk, presumably without danger. The Army Corps of Engineers had examined the seawall and found that the footings were exposed. It was hard, looking at the massive stone wall, to believe that it could really collapse, but, in fact, it had happened after the No Name Storm, when a chunk of wall, boardwalk, and fortunately no walkers, fell onto the beach. It was not a large chunk, but it gave one pause. Now there were renegades who snuck through the fence, but not many, the idea of imminent collapse being enough to scare the rest of us into model citizens. How unknowing we were the previous week when we walked on the seawall ignorantly, unafraid, watching the waves and wondering if the tide was going in or out.

After the seawall was closed, the town threw itself into a bureaucratic maelstrom in which words like *riprap* and *revetment* were bandied about willy-nilly. The Army Corps of Engineers wanted to dump a zillion pounds of small rocks below the seawall. I think, but am not sure, that this was riprap. The town countered angrily. Small rocks were nothing against the kind of wind and water this seawall saw in even a modest little storm. The engineers then suggested three-ton boulders instead of ten-pound rocks. The town was now happy, though how the boulders were going to actually get over or past the seawall onto the beach remained a point of speculation.

The large salt pond I lived on was an integral feature of the coastline of Six Mile Beach, and made frequent appearances in the town newspaper. The pond controversies included midges, widgeon grass, and salinity. What I called midges were tiny, near-invisible, biting insects, no-see-ums, but the pond was overrun with midges that looked a lot like mosquitoes and swarmed but did not bite. They seemed to leave our little corner of the pond alone during the day, but at night in the summer we had to turn off the kitchen and outside lights or they would find their way in and sit on the ceiling whining. Getting in and out of the house was preceded by reminders to shut the door rapidly, and accompanied by cries of "Quick! Quick! Quick!"

The midges had been uncontrolled for several years, proliferating in the widgeon grass. The widgeon grass ran rampant due to the lack of salinity. The lack of salinity stemmed from the pond's inability to return to its tidal past. It was once completely linked to the ocean by the same river that my ex-husband lived on. At his house, the change of tides was dramatic, the river flowing so fast in either outgoing or incoming directions that there was actually a tiny bit of white water. Now the salinity of the pond was controlled only by the opening and closing of tidal gates three times a week. A man at the end of my street opened and closed them according to the tides. This seemed like an interesting, though low-paying, job until you figured that he was ruled by the moon and had to get up in the middle of the night for days in a row every month.

Another aspect of the midge/widgeon grass/salinity problem was that what used to be an island was now attached by a land bridge. There were large conduits built into the land bridge, meant to let water circulate in and out, but they were unfortunately above water level and choked with widgeon grass. The assumption was that if circulation was restored to the pond, the widgeon grass would die, and the midges would abandon ship, so to speak. There were two voluntary groups dedicated to the restoration of the pond, which, though it belonged to the town, had been taken on as a project by the people who lived near it. It was widely rumored that one group thought too much and moved too slowly, and the other thought too little and moved too quickly. Because of its wetland status there were lots of rules about what could and could not be done with or without permits. But one morning the conduits were mysteriously free of plant material.

"You would be surprised," said a friend, "what can happen under cover of darkness."

Alice Bindle said that in Six Mile Beach you didn't have to worry about your garden and you didn't have to wear clothes that match. Sage, whose daughter-in-law grew up in Six Mile, said that its inhabitants were under a spell that made them never want to leave.

"You move there and then you don't go anywhere," she said. She said there were people in Six Mile who had never been to the city that is only a half hour away by boat. That there were people who had been to the city, but never farther. The town was full of people who grew up there, came back there, or never left. There was an undercurrent of rough pride in Six Mile Beach that ran from the hills of huge Victorians to the run-down cottages of the lowlands. Six Mile Beach inspired a kind of hunkering down. It kept a kind of secret from the people of Hearts-Are-Cold. I felt that secret as soon as I moved here. It was a secret clothed in flannel shirts and kindness and surrounded by water. It took me a little while to figure out that in spite of its connection to land, psychologically Six Mile Beach was an island.

We lived a half mile from two wealthy communities. We joked that you could tell when you passed from one town to another, even with your eyes closed. At the exact town line, the hard bumpy road of Six Mile Beach became the silky smooth road of Hearts-Are-Cold, and the houses immediately went up one or two million dollars. But if you lived in Six Mile Beach you didn't really understand why anyone would ever want to live anywhere else.

And I didn't. I was under the spell now. I was steeped in the negative ions pouring in off the ocean. My soul was finally relaxing. I was coming to my senses. Beyond the gap in the fence and the canopy formed by the two ancient apple trees, across the expanse of water, a line of gray and white cottages ringed the opposite shore. The houses themselves seemed to befriend me. Day or night I felt them, the souls of beach houses, tireless, eternal, white, gray, white, and the big water just beyond.

I got up one morning, put my daughter in the red Corvette, and sat at my kitchen table staring at the pond and letting my tea go cold. I dressed and drove to work. I parked in the parking lot and could not get out of the car.

"Don't go in there," said the voice.

"I can't just *not go in*," I said. "I am a responsible person."

So I went in, found my boss, and quit. Then I went home and took my dog to the beach, where, although the wind was cold, and brisker than usual, the walkers smiled at me, and tipped their metaphorical hats.

Summer—Fall—Winter—Spring

Winter didn't last forever after all, though it did overstay its welcome. Not until the second full week in April did I believe that it would finally, reluctantly, say goodbye. That week I sat in my new office, once the mudroom, surrounded by stacks of files and receipts, and for the first time as a newly single person lost myself for days in the rite of passage known as paying taxes. I had walked the financial plank when I quit my job, but money trickled in. I had some left, still, from the sale of our house in Hearts-Are-Cold, but as always happens, our new house had consumed more of it than planned. I took on a few private students, and my bank accounts got low but did not run dry. I was a different person than the one who used to ignore the quarter that occasionally dropped from my wallet. I picked up every nickel and dime. If a penny fell onto the ground in the grimy parking lot of the convenience store, I picked it up.

In the midst of the taxes, I stepped outside with my dog one night and discovered that the temperature had risen to about 70 degrees since sunset, and that a fine misty rain was falling. I thought, "Why, this is the salamander rain." Every year in the first warm spring rain, the salamanders come out of their winter beds to mate in the vernal pools. I had never seen them, but I knew people who had. The peepers come out that same day, and sure enough two nights later, driving through the woods, I heard their chorus.

That Saturday I opened all the windows. I hooked up the hose and cleaned out the chicken coop. I bleached and washed the feeders and waterers. I gathered all of the miscellaneous cups and bowls and small pieces of debris that had piled up in the coop's window boxes over the winter. The chickens themselves looked a bit worse for wear. Some of them had bald spots on their chests—I suspected they were pulling each other's feathers out, as chickens sometimes do, out of boredom or bossiness—and a few of them looked small to me. Months had passed since we had really spent time with them, looked at them, appreciated them. While I cleaned the winter's bedding out of the coop, Blackie and Big Yellow sat side by side in the nest box, light and dark, Zen priests, with minds like cloudless skies. Two hours later they were still there, and one of the Reds was waiting her turn, so I reached in—underneath a nesting hen is a mythically warm place—and took away their eggs.

Randall Bindle told me to wait a year before worrying about the yard. Alice told me to wait ten. Alfred puttered about cheerfully, mending benches, painting windowsills.

"Beautiful day," I called over.

"They'll be home soon," he said.

I am not a gardener. I am not a person who craves the spring or lives for the weekends, when I can putter in the flower beds. When my daughter was young we rented a plot at a local organic farm. It was about fifteen by fifteen feet, not so big. By the middle of the summer we were dispirited. Our neighbor gardens were heavy producers, tidy, weed-free, and neatly contained by railroad ties. Ours had weeds galore and zucchini the size of clubs. We were so proud of our one cantaloupe, until we ate it and realized it had cross-pollinated with a squash and had no taste at all.

So last year, in Hearts-Are-Cold, when my daughter proposed that we grow vegetables from seed, I was not enthusiastic. But I bought a hundred dollars' worth of seeds and trays, dirt and grow lamps, and peat chips that expanded into little pots when watered. We set up the seed trays and filled them with soil containing small pellets of fertilizer, one of which the dog promptly chewed and spat out. In her one year of life with us, I had already spent a fair amount of money trying to save this dog from a variety of ingested, or presumably ingested, objects. As a puppy, she climbed onto a table, over a chair, and onto the counter, where she snagged a bottle of Motrin. After an undisclosed amount of time, she ran happily into the living room, where I was reading a book, with the bottle in her mouth.

"Please don't let it be open," I said. But it was. Motrin was all over the floor, the chair, and the backyard. There was no way to count, to know, how many she might have taken.

"Come in immediately," said the woman at the twenty-four-hour animal hospital, and so we did.

Two hundred dollars and no Motrin later, we were on our way home. This was my first indication that my dog was no fool, but it would take the case of the missing earring to drive the point home. Decades of street-dog breeding had left her with discerning genes. That case would involve another trip to the vet and an X-ray, more dollars, and no sign of the earring. I felt slightly proud of her wisdom in not eating an earring, since there was a six-month-old mastiff in the waiting room who had swallowed a sock.

After the earring incident, I decided that if she could chew on a bottle of Motrin for quite some time, spurning the Motrin itself, and spit out an earring after a few bites, I would now trust her to eat anything she wanted and to spit out what wasn't good. But my daughter was terrified about the fertilizer pellet and so I called the vet.

"Come in immediately," she said. "But call the poison control center first."

I sighed, and she knew that I thought it was stupid.

"It's *poisonous*," she said disapprovingly, and gave me a phone number.

"What kind of fertilizer was this?" said the accented voice at the poison control center for animals.

I read him the label off the bag of soil.

"Does it have nitrogen?" he asked. It did not.

"What percentage of this, this, and this does it have?" he asked, giving me various chemical names. I gave him the answers.

"How much did she eat?"

"She chewed on a pellet." How big was the pellet? (Tiny.) How big was the dog? (Beagle-sized.) Did she swallow the pellet? (No.)

"She didn't eat a whole bag of this?" (No.)

"Please hold while I do the math," he said.

On hold, I was treated to a variety of extremely cheerful jazz music interspersed with cheery messages about poison control. My head was about to spin off from the strain of it, when he came back on the line.

"She will be fine," he said, repeating his name and encouraging me to call back at any time, thus adding sixty dollars, payable by credit card, to the cost of our new garden, and furthering my determination to trust this dog's wisdom in choice of food items.

I will say that expanding the peat pellets was great fun. These are similar to expandable sponges and washcloths that grow to about fifty times their initial size when immersed in water. When the peat pellets expand, one pushes a seed into the small hole at the top. Into these and the seed trays we planted our first crops: tomatoes, hot peppers, green peppers, cucumbers, and our inedible friend, the snapdragon. We felt extremely farmish, and placed the gardens in sunny windows, which were, unfortunately, within reach of the dog's gymnastic prowess. I found the first peat cup shredded on the living room couch. We moved the peat cups up a few levels. We found the next three peat cups on the living room floor and the hall rug, and we moved them up again. We did not call her our circus dog for no reason. The next time, we caught her in the act, running joyously down the hallway with a peat cup in her mouth. We were down to four cucumbers. The tomatoes and the peppers and the snapdragons sprouted, withered, and died. My mother eventually took pity on us and gave us two hardy-looking tomato plants. We planted them in the large pots, surrounded by pansies, but they did not do well, either.

This year I decided to have four raised beds and forgo the seeds. As I thought of the beds, where they would go, and when I would build them, I began to crave that garden. I would not, I understood, be happy in my house until I had that garden, and three dogwood trees in a line by the driveway, and as many peonies as I could plant. I had had a peony once, and now I thought it would be a good idea to have hundreds.

I measured out the perimeters of the beds and tried to

figure out how much lumber I would need to build them. It may have been the days of tax preparations, or the memories of other recent construction projects, but I had a hard time believing my numbers. Once I started working it out in my mind, what was the best way to do it, how many ties I would need or how many board feet of one-by-tens, I had to let it go for a while. I was two really good saws, a workshop, and a carpenter away from having fun with wood.

As for the lawn, it was terrifying in its vigor. My father had said he was going to give me his rider lawn mower since he never planned to mow a lawn again. But then he forgot, or getting it the two hours to my house was too much to think about. Suddenly, about a week after the salamander rain, the lawn was tall and I knew I would have to mow it. So I went to the hardware store in Hearts-Are-Cold and bought a lawn mower. I brought it home and mowed the lawn. It was a terrifyingly large expanse of grass, albeit flat, and though the shaded front yard did not yet require cutting, the back almost did me in.

First, I suited up: old clothes, shoes, sunglasses, ear protectors, and a new green visor I had bought at the hardware store.

"Look at my hat," I said to my daughter. She looked at the outfit.

"You've got to be kidding," she said.

Undaunted, I went outside and started the lawn mower,

and I enjoyed it for five minutes, I really did. Two hours later, still mowing, I had a wet dish towel draped over my head and water bottles in both of my pockets. I had run over a snake and three dog toys, and never wanted to see grass again.

"I bought a lawn mower," I told my mother later.

"What kind?"

"The kind you push around the lawn," I said, a bit confused.

"That was stupid," she said, and we proceeded to have an argument about push versus self-propelled, which I felt that I lost, although I did not say so. My mother was eighty years old, independent, and stubborn. She had only a few years ago set up a tall ladder, climbed it, and maced a squirrel that had the temerity to enter her garage. She complained that the squirrel still didn't leave—of course, I thought, because he was now *blind*—and I considered giving her a flame-thrower for her next birthday. I had bought the second-to-cheapest lawn mower, not really taking into account the greater benefit of having a lawn mower that would pull me rather than one I would have to push. She said the self-propelled one was only a hundred dollars more. I knew it was at least two, but I was not going to win. Regardless, I subsequently drooled over the Husqvarnas in the home improvement store, and wondered if I should get one. I didn't. I didn't want to admit defeat, and I didn't want to buy another lawn mower. So I mowed the lawn, which grew like a weed that spring. I mowed it, but not as often as I should have. I mowed it only when my dog started to have to wade through it instead of walk on it, and every time I took that lawn mower out, I thought of the self-propelled and the rider, bit down, and pushed.

A few days later my mother called to say that she had been to the farmer's market and did I want some patio tomatoes. I told her I had already bought some.

"How much did you spend?" she asked.

"Fourteen dollars," I said, thinking this was a pretty good price for two extremely large plants.

"Oh no," she said. "Oh no." It was all right to spend hundreds more on a lawn mower, but one should be frugal with tomatoes.

One day the leaves appeared on the trees, just like that, overnight, without warning. I built just one raised bed out of cedar planks and filled it with my tomatoes, tiny cucumbers, and lettuce that my mother had given me. I planted sage and rosemary and thyme in pots. I bought a wheelbarrow and a shovel, and three clematis that I planted around the footings of the deck. I planted pansies in the tub that had held the boughs of The Vengeance. I bought a climbing hydrangea for the side steps and a tree peony for my mother.

"Don't buy me any plants," she said right before Mother's Day.

"I already did," I told her.

"Well, don't," she said.

"Do you want to know what it is?" I asked.

"Okay."

"It's a tree peony." She liked tree peonies.

"I'll take it," she said.

The fence brothers came back at my request and doubled the size of the chicken run by removing all the panels and re-configuring them. My daughter helped me stretch a mile of bird netting over the top. We attached it to the run with zip ties, God's gift to the unhandy. It took the chickens a day to pull up all the grass in the new half. I had two large trash bar-rels full of what I had taken out of the coop after the long winter. The Bindles wanted as much as I would give them; they would have taken it all. You are productive girls, I told the chickens, and gave them an extra piece of bread and five worms.

A few days later I found myself at the feed store just after new chicks had arrived. "Do not pick up," said the sign, and I didn't want to. I wanted to watch them and think how much things change when they grow up and how unex-pected it all is. The chicks flapped and tried to fly. I could pick out the Araucanas and the Light Brahmas. Some of them had an unpleasant but easily remedied condition called pasty butt, which is, unfortunately, just what it sounds like.

"They're out of water," I told the woman.

"They have water," she said officiously, which made me mad.

I pointed to the empty water font. "And some of them have pasty butt," I said. And then I swept, regally, knowledgeably, out of the store.

By spring my daughter fully inhabited her teenage self. She had inherited the clotheshorse gene from her father, though not the conservative gene, and she dressed in an astonishingly fashionable, thrown together, interesting way. She took a course in fashion design and pored over the summer and fall collections for inspiration. One day she appeared in the kitchen, her hands full of pages ripped out of fashion magazines. "You are not going to believe this," she said, shaking her head in disgust. "*Leopard* is the new black."

For Easter she wore, to my mother-in-law's country club, white capris, a red-and-black Paris T-shirt, the black linen peplum jacket, black-and-hot-pink-striped thigh-high socks, and lime-green slip-on sandals. She pulled it off. Her hair was cut in a French bob. She was gorgeous. No one could take their eyes off her. When she left for four days on a sailing schooner with her class, four days in which she would not be able to shower, wash her hair, or preen, she dressed carefully in layers that could be removed without ruining the effect, put an orange baseball cap on backward, spritzed the air twice with perfume, walked through, put on a pair of baby blue sunglasses, and was ready. But true to her spirit, when her friends gathered up their belongings and carried them efficiently to the boat, my daughter trailed behind, her raincoat off one shoulder, her daypack off another, dragging her duffle and carrying her sleeping bag. She looked like a gypsy.

In spite of the fact that I had grown stodgy in her eyes, I was *cool* for about a day in April because my daughter's favorite alternative rock station mentioned some bands that were playing in an uber-hip city club, and I said I had been to it.

"You're kidding. When?"

"I don't know," I said. "In my early thirties, I suppose."

Later, after talking on the phone for the requisite hours to her best friend, she said, "You're her hero."

"Why?"

"Because you used to go to that club, and because you wrote poetry and gave readings and people took black-and-white pictures of you, and you were people's muse. And I have to admit," she continued, "that I used to think that you were sort of born my mother, like you are now, but now I realize that you really did have a life before that."

I myself had to stretch sometimes to remember that I actually had that life as a wild girl. I found it ironic that part of my occupation now was to educate and worry about that wild girl's wild daughter, her teenage self, her adventures in the world. All I wanted was for her to be safe and sober and happy, but life is also made of danger and intoxication and sorrow. She would not have a plain vanilla life, this girl who was not afraid of ugliness or difference, and so I should just learn some other skill. "I am confident in you," I practiced. "You are capable and make good choices."

Later, she told the story of my coolness to F., who popped the bubble. "Yeah, my dad was really cool in high school," she said. "What the hell happened to *him*?"

Cool or not, life went on. And one day late in May, when it was alternately too cold and too hot, when Phoebe was expanding her lawn reclamation project, and Randall was spraying weed killer on poison ivy, a mockingbird spent the day in my yard singing. He never stopped all day, shifting from birdsong to birdsong, never repeating. He had other sounds in his repertoire, some that sounded like owls or tiny foghorns. And it was impossible not to laugh listening to him shift from one song to another.

"He's showing off," said my daughter, and I thought he was right to, showing how worldly he was, how far he had come, what he now knew that he wasn't born knowing.

Zen Chickens

Some days it is hard to say just what is so attractive about chickens. They are not the cleanest of creatures. They are poor housekeepers. They are sometimes mean. They constitute a farm chore. More than other animals, in my experience, with chickens there's always something. Something wrong with the coop, the roost is too low, the ventilation inadequate. You run out of bedding. You run out of food. You run out of grit, or scratch, or sunflower seeds. They need more protein, they need more calcium, they need more grass. They get dirty, or they get worms, or mites, or fungus. Their toes fall off. Their beaks fall off. Their feet fall off. Their combs fall off. One famous chicken, Mike the Headless Chicken, lived for eighteen months without a *head*. He has his own Web site. Otherwise everything that can go wrong seems to. The crop impacts, the vent prolapses, the eggs go spongy. And everything, *everything*, wants to eat them.

I had enemies now, fox, raccoon, possum, coyote. I kept

a close eye on dogs, though most of them were surprisingly uninterested. The only dogs who were unfailingly and keenly interested in killing my chickens were huskies, and Six Mile Beach seemed to be stuffed with them. The Bindles had two. The lady in the red Corvette had *seven*. Even the mythical white husky from Porrazzo Road had made an appearance at my coop. He wanted to eat the chickens immediately. He was also clearly a dog that had enjoyed too much freedom and was skilled at evading capture. I chased him out of the yard with a rake, but he came back. The chickens were terrified. I picked up a rock. I cannot throw, hit, or catch, and I have been a miserable failure at baseball my whole life, but I hit that moving white husky in the side with my rock from a distance of fifteen feet. I don't think it hurt him in the least, but it made him think, and off he ran. I made the mistake of bragging about it for a while, until I realized that anyone who didn't have chickens considered hitting a dog with a rock pretty despicable. Then I only bragged about it online, where I had become one of those people whose response to any varmint quandary was, "Shoot it."

But one night, I woke from a sound sleep, sat up, looked out the window, and saw a black coyote, the size of a large wolf, bound across my large backyard in four or five huge leaps, and disappear into the shadows. I would not see another one for a long time, but I never let the dog out alone at night again. She could run, and she was fast, but at heart she was a chicken, and the chickens were sitting ducks. I didn't want that coyote around, and feared him and his kind, and knew what he could do to me and my animals, and hated the worry he had just added to my life. But the two seconds in which he bounded across my life changed my thinking forever. He was too beautiful and free to hate.

So what was it about chickens that made me want to set up my lawn chair out there by the chicken yard, sit down with a glass of lemonade, and watch? They are simple. They don't seem to think much. Their minds are like the clear blue skies the meditation teachers tell us to have. "The thoughts come in, let them float away, like clouds. . . ." Chickens really *have* that kind of mind. I didn't know how big their brains are, but I don't think there is room for too many clouds in there at once.

And although the chickens were busy, they were not in a hurry. They were calming. They were funny, although they had no sense of humor. They puttered, but in a serious sort of way. Chickens take themselves very seriously, actually. They have a sort of mindless gravitas. I could almost see them as members of a monastery, deliberate. But also random, like idiots. Having watched chickens for a good amount of time in the course of their short lifetime with us, I had seen a certain repetition of thought and action.

Worry. And then don't. Look, a goose. If someone else has it, check it out because it might be good. Or it could just be a stick. If she comes out of the house, she might have bread. Oh no. She doesn't. When you lay an egg, make noise about it. If there's some-one in the nest, go in there anyway. The dog is eating grass on the other side of the fence? Go on. Stick your head out there. Peck the dog's tongue. It might be a worm. Jesus Christ, it's the lawn mower. Eat almost anything. When it gets dark, go inside. Huddle up. Everything is exciting. Fly when you can.

At dusk, after I shooed them through the door with a dish towel, they huddled up in the corner between the chicken door and the human door. At that point I could pet them all, even the skittish ones. They were quiet and not asleep yet, but they had achieved an altered state. Transcendent, I thought.

Once, when I entered the coop late in the evening, when I had put them in but not closed the windows, I found them walking slowly, in a loosely held circle, crooning. I felt like I had entered the location of a primitive rite, in which the se-cret life of chickens was revealed to me. They looked like Zen monks in walking meditation, and I remembered a meditation teacher I once had, whose eyes had a strange glow that looked suspiciously like a dragon's, or, as I now re-alized, like a chicken's. I saw the same oddly intelligent rep-tilian glow as one of the Reds peered at me as if to calculate my worthiness.

And so I began to think of the chickens as Buddhas. I had taken to reading the *Tao Te Ching*, seeking some spiritual wisdom, and really, just about everything in there could have been written about a chicken.

That which has no substance enters where there is no space.

Let your workings remain a mystery.

Those who know don't talk.

I didn't think that the inverse was true, that silence bred knowledge. I was not much of a talker, really, and I knew next to nothing. I had been thinking about the meaning of life for months and had gotten nowhere. It was a fruitless, fruitless endeavor, and none of the answers I came up with was at all inspiring or held any grace, yet I did it anyway. I had a boyfriend once who, before I knew him, had become convinced that one of his friends was Jesus and that the others were the disciples. Okay, he was crazy. But the point is that when I asked him how he got out of it, he said that he didn't, he just didn't let himself think about it much anymore.

Blackie died egg-bound on the first day of summer, the day before the hollyhocks bloomed, and it took the heart out of me a little. Maybe it was because of my father's failing health, as some suggested, or maybe it was that too much had been lost, or that I was alone. Maybe it was just that she was a good chicken and my favorite and there was nothing I could do to help her. We had followed the path of those chickens, against all logic, and losing this one, the little surviving ink blot, the smart and curious Blackie, the first to try a new thing, the last to go in at night, the most independent of chickens, was too much to bear.

I was not a religious person and I did not go to church but once every few years. For most of my life I had been deeply moved by the beauty of the world, in which I found all the transcendent moments I needed. But now I decided that I needed to talk to people about death because lately there had been too many endings. My list of people to ask included friends and other people I knew, as well as people I had seen around who I thought might know something, like the Unitarian minister from Hearts-Are-Cold who once sang the reggae version of "By the Rivers of Babylon" in the middle of a sermon. I thought of asking the mother of one of my daughter's classmates, a deeply spiritual and Catholic woman who seemed to radiate comfort.

Then I remembered that two days earlier, dropping my daughter off at this woman's house for the birthday party of her son, a large blonde stranger came up to my car and began talking about my dog, who was in the backseat with her head out the window. She said how blessed we were to have these creatures and that they were gifts from God. She said that she had put her dog down the previous Tuesday. As I began to offer my condolences, she interrupted me.

"No, no," she said. "It was so beautiful." She said she had buried him in her front yard and that her neighbors—she had not planned this—came over and played clarinets.

"God is good," she said. "I am moving through God all the time. I am *swimming* in God," she said, waving her arms.

"Do you know how I know?" she asked.

I didn't.

"I know because the world is made of protons," she said, "and God is in every one of them. Every single one of them, and wherever I go . . ." She waved her arms in the swimming motion again.

She was bold and cheerful and brilliantly not just talking. She was walking the walk. She was spreading the news, and it didn't matter, not to me or to her, that I didn't believe what she did, or do what she did about it, or know at the time just what she was giving me that I would soon need.

I gave our sister Blackie back to the earth, where her protons would join in the joyous dance of whatever-it-is, and I thanked her. I told her she was a good chicken and that we loved her and that she gave us joy. I realized what the chickens had given us, way back then, when it made no sense to get them and we got them anyway. They had given us hope, and maybe that's all there is. Maybe that's what Yo-Yo Ma gives us, and Bach, and Puccini, and the faces of our children, our friends, our families, good work, the ocean, the moon rising over the pond, the havens of our homes. I had followed the chickens this far and would follow them farther. They were still talking to me, singing to me, telling me a story.

Dragonfly Farm

My expensive shoes were ruined. The stiff leather work gloves I bought when I built the ark were battered and stained, and when I took them off they retained the shape of my hands. They had small rips and tears in the now-soft, thick leather, from chicken wire and hardware cloth and tree limbs and tools. At least two of the fingers had old Band-Aids permanently fused into the tips. It was a long way I had traveled since I had been stunned into motion by the circumstances of my life.

I remembered driving home from the granary with six chicks in a cardboard box, the saunalike heat of the bathroom, and sitting on the floor of the bathroom with baby chickens flying madly all around me. I remembered signing my house away, crying, the bloom of the apple tree. I remembered standing by the refrigerator box in the middle of the night and classical music playing. I remembered walking into the lawyer's office in my grubby clothes with my dog on a leash. I remembered the drywall falling, the first flood, the second flood, a jade-green egg. I remembered sitting at the kitchen table talking about marriage with the electricians while they installed the microwave. The midnight drives to the super-market. Greasing the combs. The Vengeance. The party. The first storm. The day I left my job. The boardwalk. Blackie. And through it all and above all, my daughter and companion, and the friends and family who helped us through.

Now it was summer. There were days when the fog rolled in off the ocean and blew right through the open windows of my kitchen in clouds. There were days when it was 20 de-grees colder at my house than a mile away in Hearts-Are-Cold. The pond was full of swans, overpopulated, really. We once counted over fifty of them, bobbing like corks in the blue water. And, lured by dozens of floating birdhouses, wood swallows took up residence on the pond. During the day we could see them, whirling and wheeling on pointed wings. One hoped they were eating midges.

The Bindles built a new raised bed and Phoebe bought lemon thyme and ripped up more of her lawn. Mr. G. walked around his yard setting off firecrackers to scare the grackles out of his cherry trees. My daughter was the breakout star of the school musical and planned her graduation outfit. My fa-ther raced his sailboats and slowly lost his breath.

At night it was still quieter than I could imagine it being

and I still often woke up and looked out the window, across the expanse of my land, to the woods beyond, and across the pond, where the lights in some of the cottages were on all night and reflected in the water. In the silence of the darkness was something that I didn't expect to find when I decided to buy the small sad house in Six Mile Beach. I had thought I was renovating a house. I didn't know that in the process I would also rebuild my life.

Perfection did not visit me. The meaning of life was not simple. I didn't know, that day in January, when I decided that I would have to sell my house in Hearts-Are-Cold, that grace lay in wait on a six-mile beach. I did not have a year in Provence or a villa under the Tuscan sun. I did not have a farm in Africa. It turned out that my life was not someone else's book. It was not a picture and it was not still. It was moving, variegated, unpredictable. It was a life, with chickens.

ACKNOWLEDGMENTS

This book was started by accident over a bathtub full of chickens and finished on purpose in the library of the Rhode Island School of Design, which is at the top of a very steep hill. There are a hundred people behind this book, unseen by the reader, but not by my heart. This is where I get to thank them.

To my agent, Liv Blumer, who believed in this book and its author from the beginning. For her intelligence and humor and vision and courage, I will always be grateful.

To my editor, Laureen Rowland, publisher and founder of Hudson Street Press, for her enthusiasm and for taking on this book with love. It has been a pleasure all the way.

To Clare Ferraro, president of Plume; Kathryn Court, publisher of Plume; and Trena Keating, associate publisher at Plume, for welcoming *Still Life with Chickens* into paperback.

To Danielle Friedman, assistant editor at Hudson Street Press, for her work on this book in cloth and paperback editions. And to Elizabeth Keenan, associate director of publicity for Hudson Street Press and Plume, and Marie Coolman, director of marketing and publicity for Hudson Street Press and Plume, for their belief in this book and all of their many efforts on its behalf.

To Suzanne Gluck and a raft of other agents, whose enthusiasm and encouragement lifted my spirits along the way.

To Wes in Texas and the chicken masters of Backyard Chickens, who got us through.

To the men who made it possible, my white knights: John, Rick, Rich, and Doug.

To our family of friends called "Marshfield," without whom our lives would be so much poorer, I bow in thanks a thousand times and still that is not enough.

To Paula Duggins, Janet Brady, and Pam Hoffman, for the lambent light.

To my friends Suzanne Cox and Marion Webster, for their love and support and wisdom. And to Barbara Green, for more than I can say.

To Sue Lofchie, Linda Ferrier and Lawry Reed, and Mr. and Mrs. G., for bordering Dragonfly Farm with goodness, and to Six Mile Beach for taking us in. And to our friends and neighbors in the town I call Hearts-Are-Cold, whose hearts are made of gold.

To Anna Carr, mother, gardener, quilter, friend, for the example of a life well lived. To Chip Rutan for his humor and intelligence, wisdom, and support. To Bill Rutan, for his stalwart, artistic soul.

To my father, who I have to believe can read this from heaven.

To Richard Goldhammer, friend and family, always.

To Sam, Monkey, and the winged Buddhas.

And most of all to Emma. How lucky I am to be your mother, ever amazed and grateful for your presence in my life.